BY ALEKSANDR SOLZHENITSYN

REBUILDING
RUSSIA

ALEKSANDR SOLZHENITSYN

REBUILDING RUSSIA

REFLECTIONS

AND

TENTATIVE

PROPOSALS

▼

Translated and annotated by
ALEXIS KLIMOFF

Farrar, Straus and Giroux
New York

Library of Congress Cataloging-in-Publication Data
Solzhenitsyn, Aleksandr Isaevich.
Rebuilding Russia: reflections and tentative proposals /
Aleksandr Solzhenitsyn ; translated from the Russian by Alexis
Klimoff. —1st ed.
p. cm.
1. Soviet Union—Politics and government—1985–   2.   Soviet Union—
Economic policy—1986–   3.   Perestroïka—Soviet Union.   I. Title.
DK288.S636   1991   320.947   dc20
91-29983   CIP

Rebuilding Russia was written in July 1990
and was first published in the U.S.S.R. in
September 1990 as "How to Revitalize Russia,"
in *Komsomolskaya Pravda*, among the country's
largest circulation dailies.

CONTENTS

CONTENTS

FIRST

PRIORITIES

Time has finally run out for communism.

But its concrete edifice has not yet crumbled.

And we must take care not to be crushed beneath its rubble instead of gaining liberty.

AT THE END OF OUR ENDURANCE

Can there still be anyone among us who is unaware of our troubles, covered up though they are by mendacious statistics? For seventy years in labored pursuit of a purblind and malignant Marxist–Leninist utopia, we have lost a full third of our population—lives yielded up to the

executioner or squandered in the ineptly, almost suici-
dally waged "Patriotic War."[1] We have forfeited our earlier abundance, destroyed the peasant class together
with its settlements, deprived the raising of crops of its
whole purpose and the soil of its ability to yield a har-
vest, while flooding the land with man-made seas and
swamps. The environs of our cities are befouled by the
effluents of our primitive industry, we have poisoned our
rivers, lakes, and fish, and today we are obliterating our
last resources of clean water, air, and soil, speeding the
process by the addition of nuclear death, further supple-
mented by the storage of Western radioactive wastes
for money. Depleting our natural wealth for the sake of
grandiose future conquests under a crazed leadership,
we have cut down our luxuriant forests and plundered
our earth of its incomparable riches—the irreplaceable
inheritance of our great-grandchildren—in order to sell
them off abroad with uncaring hand. We have saddled
our women with backbreaking, impossibly burdensome
labor, torn them from their children, and have abandoned the children themselves to disease, brutishness,
and a semblance of education. Our health care is utterly
neglected, there are no medicines, and we have even
forgotten the meaning of a proper diet. Millions lack
housing, and a helplessness bred of the absence of personal rights permeates the entire country. And through-

out all this we cling to only one thing: that we not be deprived of unlimited drunkenness.

Human beings are so constituted that we can put up with such ruination and madness even when they last a lifetime, but God forbid that anyone should dare to offend or slight our *nationality*! Should that occur, nothing can restrain us in our state of chronic submission: with furious courage we snatch up stones, clubs, spears, and guns and fall upon our neighbors, intent on murder and arson. Such is man: nothing has the capacity to convince us that our hunger, our poverty, our early deaths, the degeneration of our children—that any of these misfortunes can take precedence over national pride.

And that is why, in this attempt to propose some tentative steps toward our recovery and reconstruction, we are forced to begin, not with our unendurable wounds or debilitating suffering, but with a response to such questions as: How will the problem of the nationalities be approached? And within what geographical boundaries shall we heal our afflictions or die? And only thereafter shall we turn to the healing process itself.

WHAT IS RUSSIA?

The word "Russia" has become soiled and tattered through careless use; it is invoked freely in all sorts of inappropriate contexts. Thus, when the monster-like U.S.S.R. was lunging for chunks of Asia and Africa, the reaction the world over was: "Russia, the Russians . . ."

What exactly *is* Russia? Today, now? And—more important—tomorrow? Who, today, considers himself part of the future Russia? And where do Russians themselves see the boundaries of their land?

In the course of three-quarters of a century, to the sound of incessant proclamations trumpeting "the socialist friendship of peoples," the communist regime has managed to neglect, entangle, and sully the relationship among these peoples to such a degree that one can no longer see the way back to the peaceful coexistence of nationalities, that almost drowsy non-perception of distinctions that had virtually been achieved—with some lamentable exceptions—in the final decades of pre-revolutionary Russia. For all that, it may not yet be too late to sort things out and come to an understanding—but not in the midst of the grievous misfortunes that are tearing at us with hurricane strength. From the vantage point of today, the more peaceful resolution, and the one holding much greater promise for the future, calls for a decisive parting of the ways for those who should separate. This is precisely due to the all-pervading ethnic bitterness that has obscured the rest of life: all else seems unimportant in the grip of a passion to which few of our people are immune.

Many of us know only too well, alas, that sharing a communal apartment can at times make life itself seem intolerable. And that is exactly how inflamed things have become in our national interrelationships.

In many of the republics at the periphery, centrifugal forces have built up such momentum that they could not be stopped without violence and bloodshed—*nor should they be checked at such cost.* The way things are moving in our country, the "Soviet Socialist Union" will break up *whatever* we do: we have no real choice, there is nothing to ponder, and it remains only to bestir ourselves in order to forestall greater misfortunes and to assure that the separation proceeds without needless human suffering and only in those cases where it is truly unavoidable.

As I see it, it must be declared loudly, clearly, and without delay that the three republics in the Baltic area, the three in Transcaucasia, four in Central Asia, and Moldavia as well, if it feels drawn to Romania—that these eleven will be *separated off unequivocally and irreversibly.*[2] (On the process of separation itself, see below.)

As for Kazakhstan, its present huge territory was stitched together by the communists in a completely haphazard fashion: wherever migrating herds made a yearly passage would be called Kazakhstan. But then drawing boundaries was not considered important in those years, since we were supposedly but a short moment away from the time when all nationalities would merge into one. And Lenin in his perceptive way referred to boundaries as an issue "perhaps ten points down on the scale of priorities." (That is why they sliced the Nagorno-Karabakh region into Azerbaijan. What difference did it make where it went? What was important at the time was to play up to Turkey, that great friend of the Soviets.[3]) And in any case Kazakhstan was considered an Autonomous Republic within the R.S.F.S.R. until 1936, when it was promoted to Union Republic status.[4] It had been assembled from southern Siberia and the southern Ural region, plus the sparsely populated central areas which had since that time been transformed and built up by Russians, by inmates of forced-labor camps, and by exiled peoples.[5] Today the Kazakhs constitute noticeably less than half the population of the entire inflated territory of Kazakhstan. They are concentrated in their long-standing ancestral domains along a large arc of lands in the south, sweeping from the extreme east westward almost to the Caspian Sea; the population here is indeed predominantly Kazakh. And if it should prove to be their wish to separate within such boundaries, I say Godspeed.

And so, after subtracting these twelve republics, there will remain nothing but an entity that might be called Rus, as it was designated in olden times (the word "Russian" had for centuries embraced Little Russians [Ukrainians], Great Russians, and Belorussians), or else "Russia," a name used since the eighteenth century, or—for an accurate reflection of the new circumstances—the "Russian [*Rossiiskii*] Union."[6]

But even then such an entity would contain a hundred different nationalities and ethnic groups ranging in size from the tiny to the very considerable.[7] And this is the very threshold from which we can and must manifest great wisdom and understanding. Only from that moment on must we marshal all the resources of our hearts and minds to the task of consolidating a fruitful commonwealth of nations, affirming the integrity of each culture and the preservation of each language.

A WORD TO THE GREAT RUSSIANS

At the beginning of this century the eminent political thinker Sergei Kryzhanovsky foresaw that "the Russian heartland does not possess the reserves of cultural and moral strength necessary to assimilate the peripheries. That [effort] weakens the Russian national core."

And this statement was made in a rich, flourishing

country, before the extermination of millions of our people, an extermination, moreover, that was no blind mass killing, but rather involved a specific targeting of the *best* that Russia had produced.

Today Kryzhanovsky's words are a thousand times more valid: *We don't have the strength* for the peripheries either economically or morally. *We don't have the strength* for sustaining an empire—and it is just as well. Let this burden fall from our shoulders: it is crushing us, sapping our energy, and hastening our demise.

I note with alarm that the awakening Russian national self-awareness has to a large extent been unable to free itself of great-power thinking and of imperial delusions, that it has taken over from the communists the fraudulent and contrived notion of "Soviet patriotism," and that it takes pride in the "Soviet superpower" which during the reign of the dull-witted Brezhnev sucked dry what remained of our productivity for the sake of a massive and needless buildup of weapons (which, never used, are now being destroyed). Proud of the "superpower" status that brought shame upon us, presenting us to the whole world as a brutal, insatiable, and unbridled aggressor at a time when our knees were beginning to shake and weakness was bringing us to the verge of collapse. What a pernicious perversion of consciousness it is to argue that, "for all that, we are a huge country and we are taken seriously everywhere." Such an attitude now, when we are close to death, constitutes nothing less than a wholehearted support of communism. Was not Japan able to find a way to be reconciled with its situation, renouncing its sense of international mission and the pursuit of tempting political ventures—and did not that country flourish as a result?

The time has come for an uncompromising *choice* between an empire of which we ourselves are the primary victims and the spiritual and physical salvation of our own people. It is common knowledge that our mortality rate is increasing and has passed our birthrate: if this continues, we shall disappear from the face of the earth. Holding on to a great empire means to contribute to the extinction of our own people. And, anyway, what need is there of this heterogeneous amalgam? Do we want Russians to lose their unique characteristics? We must strive, not for the expansion of the state, but for a clarity of what remains of our spirit. By separating off twelve republics, by this seeming sacrifice, Russia will in fact free itself for a precious *inner* development, at long last turning diligent attention toward itself. Besides, what hope can there be of preserving and developing Russian culture amid the chaotic jumble of today? Less and less, surely, as things become ever more mashed and pounded together.

It is regrettable that our staunch and admirable Russian emigration has clung to the mirage of a "one and undivided Russia" throughout seventy years of poverty and travail. A person of such views back in 1914 would have claimed Poland as "ours," too, and would have considered it impossible to "give it up." (It had been the fatuous whim of Alexander I to make Poland happy by his patronage.) But who would insist on this point today? Did Russia lose out through the separation of Poland and Finland?[8] Quite the contrary: it only helped the country to straighten its back. And, in the same way, it will be able to straighten up even more once it has shed the onerous burden of the Central Asian "underbelly," that equally ill-considered conquest of Alexander II, who would have been far wiser to invest those energies in completing his unfinished series of reforms, and in setting up a truly representative elective assembly [*zemstvo*].

The twentieth-century Russian philosopher Ivan Ilyin has written that the spiritual life of a nation is more important than the size of its territory or even its economic prosperity; the health and happiness of the people is of incomparably greater value than any external goal based on prestige.

And, in any case, our peripheries already *are* falling

away. Surely we must not wait until the uncontrollable flood of refugees from these areas reaches the millions.

We must stop reciting like parrots: "We are proud to be Russian." "We are proud of our immense motherland." "We are proud . . ." It is time we understood that *after* all the things of which we are so justifiably proud our people gave in to the spiritual catastrophe of 1917 (and, more broadly, of 1915–32). Since then, we have become almost pathetically unlike our former selves. No longer can we be so presumptuous in our plans for the future as to dream of restoring the might and eminence of the former Russia. When our fathers and grandfathers threw down their weapons during a deadly war, deserting the front in order to plunder their neighbor at home, they in effect *made a choice* for us, with consequences for one century so far, but who knows, maybe for two. Nor can we take pride in the Soviet–German war in which we lost over thirty million men, ten times more than the enemy, while at the same time strengthening the despotism over us. "Taking pride" is not what we need to do, nor should we be attempting to impose ourselves on the lives of others. We must, rather, grasp the reality of the acute and debilitating illness that is affecting our people, and pray to God that He grant us recovery, along with the wisdom to achieve it.

And if it is true that Russia has for decades been giving its life blood to the republics, then the separation will not produce economic losses for us, but will instead allow us to conserve physical strength.

A WORD TO THE UKRAINIANS
AND THE BELORUSSIANS

I am well-nigh half Ukrainian by birth, and I grew up to the sound of Ukrainian speech. And I spent the greater part of my front-line service in sorrowful Belorussia, where I became poignantly attached to its melancholy, sparse landscape and its gentle people.

Thus, I am addressing both nations not as an outsider but *as one of their own.*

And, in any case, our people came to be divided into three branches by the terrible calamity of the Mongol invasion, and by Polish colonization.[9] All the talk of a separate Ukrainian people existing since something like the ninth century and possessing its own non-Russian language is a recently invented falsehood. We all sprang from precious Kiev, from which "the Russian land took its beginning" (as Nestor puts it in his chronicle),[10] and from which we received the light of Christianity. The same princes ruled over all of us: Yaroslav the Wise apportioned Kiev, Novgorod, and the entire expanse stretching from Chernigov to Ryazan, Murom, and Beloozero among his sons; Vladimir Monomakh was simultaneously Prince of Kiev and Prince of Rostov and Suzdal;[11] the administration of the Church exhibited the same kind of unity. The Muscovite state was of course created by the same people who made up Kievan Rus. And the Ukrainians and Belorussians in Poland and Lithuania considered themselves Russian and resisted Polonization and conversion to Catholicism. The return of these lands to Russia was at the time universally perceived as an act of *reunification*.

It is indeed painful and humiliating to recall the directives issued during the reign of Alexander II (in 1863 and 1876), when the use of the Ukrainian language was banned, first in journalism and then in belles-lettres as well. But this prohibition did not remain in force for long, and it was an example of the unenlightened rigidity in questions of administrative and Church policy that prepared the ground for the collapse of the Russian state structure.

However, it is also true that the fussily socialistic Ukrainian Rada of 1917 was created by an agreement among politicians and was not elected by popular vote.[12] And when the Rada broke with the federation, declaring the Ukraine's secession from Russia, it did so without soliciting the opinion of the population at large.

I have had occasion to respond to émigré Ukrainian nationalists who keep trying to convince America that "communism is a myth; it is really the Russians who are seeking world domination, not the communists" (and, indeed, it is "the Russians" who are supposed to have seized China and Tibet, as is stated in a law passed by the U.S. Senate three decades ago, and still on the books). [13] Communism is the kind of *myth* of which both Russians and Ukrainians got a firsthand taste in the torture chambers of the Cheka from 1918 onward. The kind of *myth* that confiscated even seed grain in the Volga region and brought twenty-nine drought-ridden Russian provinces to the murderous famine of 1921–22. The same *myth* that later thrust the Ukraine into the similarly pitiless famine of 1932–33. As common victims of the communist-imposed collectivization forced upon us all by whip and bullet, have we not been bonded by this common bloody suffering?

As late as 1848, Galicians in Austria–Hungary referred to their national council as the "Chief Russian Rada." But then in a severed Galicia, and with active Austrian encouragement, a distorted Ukrainian language was produced, unrelated to popular usage and chock-full of German and Polish words. This was followed by the attempt to force Carpatho–Russians away from their habit of using the Russian language, and by the temptations of radical Pan–Ukrainian separatism, which manifests itself among the leaders of today's emigration in bursts of farcical ignorance (such as the assertion that St. Vladimir "was a Ukrainian")[14] or reaches lunatic vehemence in statements such as: "Let communism live so long as the Muscovites perish."

How can we fail to share the pain and anguish over the mortal torments that befell the Ukraine in the Soviet period? But does that justify the ambition to lop the Ukraine off from a living organism (including those regions which have never been part of the traditional Ukraine: the "wild steppe" of the nomads—the later "New Russia"—as well as the Crimea, the Donbas area,[15] and the lands stretching east almost to the Caspian Sea)? If we are to take the "self-determination of peoples" seriously, then it follows that a nation must determine its fate *for itself*. It is a question that cannot be decided without a national plebiscite.

To separate off the Ukraine today would mean to cut across the lives of millions of individuals and families: the two populations are thoroughly intermingled; there are entire regions where Russians predominate; many individuals would be hard put to choose between the two nationalities; many others are of mixed origin, and there are plenty of mixed marriages (marriages which have indeed never been viewed as "mixed"). There is not even a hint of intolerance between Russians and Ukrainians on the level of the ordinary people.

Brothers! We have no need of this cruel partition. The very idea comes from the darkening of minds brought on by the communist years. Together we have borne the suffering of the Soviet period, together we have tumbled into this pit, and together, too, we shall find our way out.

An impressive roster of prominent names has been produced at the intersection of our two cultures over the last two centuries. As Mikhail Dragomanov has phrased it, the cultures are "indivisible, yet unmixable." An avenue must be opened—amicably and joyfully—for the free manifestation of Ukrainian and Belorussian cultures not only on their two territories but among the Great Russians as well. No forced Russification (but no forced Ukrainization either, as began in the late 1920s). There must be an untrammeled development of parallel cultures and school instruction in either language, according to the parents' choice.

Of course, if the Ukrainian people should *genuinely wish* to separate, no one would dare to restrain them by force. But the area is very heterogeneous indeed, and only the *local* population can determine the fate of a particular locality, while every ethnic minority created by this process in a given district must count upon the same kind of forbearance toward itself.

All the above holds fully for Belorussia as well, except that the passions of separatist extremism have never been stirred up in that land.

And finally let us bow our heads before the Ukraine and Belorussia in recognition of the Chernobyl disaster. It was brought about by the careerists and fools generated by the Soviet system, and we must help set things right to the extent that we are able to do so.

A WORD TO THE SMALLER NATIONALITIES AND ETHNIC GROUPS

Even after all the separations, our state will inevitably remain a multicultural one, despite the fact that this is not a goal we wish to pursue.

For substantial groups like the Tatar, Bashkir, Udmurt, Komi, Chuvash, Mordva, Mari, and Yakut peoples, there would seem to be virtually no choice, because it is simply impractical for one state to exist when it is surrounded on all sides by a second one. Other national territories will have an external border, and if they should wish to separate, no impediment can be placed in their way. (There is the added difficulty that in some Autonomous Republics the indigenous population constitutes a minority.) But on the condition that all their unique national characteristics—culture, religion, and economic structure—are preserved, it may make sense for them to remain in the union.

As the creation of many small state structures in the twentieth century shows, a great burden is placed on them in terms of supporting a plethora of governmental agencies, diplomatic missions, and armies; the process also cuts them off from large territories that provide outlets for trade and public activity. Thus, the mountain people of the Caucasus, a group distinguished by their loyalty to the Russian throne before the Revolution, will no doubt wish to weigh carefully the advantages and disadvantages of separation. It is not the large Russian Union that needs to have the smaller peripheral nations joined to itself; it is, rather, they who may have the greater need to join up. Should they wish to be with us, more credit to them.

The deliberately deceptive and mendacious Soviet system nonetheless contains some elements that have validity if they are honestly applied. One of these is the Soviet [i.e., Council] of Nationalities, [16] a forum in which even the smallest of national groups can have its voice heard. The present hierarchical structure is also justified: "Union Republics" first, followed by "Autonomous Republics," then "Autonomous Oblasts," and "National Okrugs." The numerical weight of a people must not be ignored; disregarding this factor is the road to chaos:

the UN might be able to subsist in this fashion, but not a viable state.

The Crimean Tatars must obviously be permitted to return to the Crimean peninsula.[17] But given the expected population density of the next century, the Crimea can accommodate some eight to ten million inhabitants, and the hundred-thousand-strong Tatar people cannot then demand control of the entire territory.

There are, finally, the smallest national groups: the Nenets, Permyak, Evenki, Mansi, Khakas, Chukchi, Koryak, and other peoples I cannot enumerate here. They all lived well in the Tsarist "prison of peoples" and it is we, the communist Soviet Union, who have dragged them toward extinction. There is no calculating the wrongs they have suffered from our infamous administration and from our mindless and rapacious industry, which has brought pollution and ruin into their lands, destroying support systems especially vital for the survival of critically small groups. We must lose no time in offering our help in restoring them to life and vigor. It is not yet too late.

Every people, even the very smallest, represents a unique facet of God's design. As Vladimir Solovyov has written, paraphrasing the Christian commandment: "You must love all other people as you love your own."

The twentieth century continues to be convulsed and

warped by a politics that has liberated itself from all moral criteria. States and statesmen are routinely exempted from what would be expected of any decent individual. It is high time to seek loftier forms of statehood, based not only on self-interest but also on compassion.

THE PROCESS OF SEPARATION

Thus the indisputable right of the aforementioned twelve republics to full secession must be proclaimed immediately and firmly. But what if some of them should hesitate over this question? With the same resolve we—that is, those remaining—will then need to proclaim *our* separation from them. The parting of the ways is long overdue, the process is irreversible, and the situation will only keep exploding in unpredictable places. It is plain to all that we cannot live together. So let us not keep straining under this mutual burden.

The painful and costly process of separation will make the beginning of the transitional period, that first phase of our new development, an especially difficult time for us: funds and more funds will be needed, funds that are already unavailable. But nothing less than such a separation will clear our view of the future.

Of course, the actual physical separation will not be

accomplished by any quick declaration. Any abrupt unilateral action would result in injury to countless human lives and in mutual economic ruin. There must be no resemblance to the Portuguese flight from Angola, when that country was abandoned to chaos and to years of civil war. Once separation is declared, panels of experts representing all concerned parties must begin deliberations. At this point we should also keep in mind the irresponsibly haphazard way in which the Soviet demarcation of borders was carried out. In some localities, more accurate lines may need to be drawn in order to reflect the actual population patterns; other areas might require local plebiscites under impartial supervision.

This sorting process might well take several years.

Millions of people will be faced with the difficult question of whether to stay where they had been living or to move away. The latter option will entail a disruption of their life in its entirety, beginning with their physical setting, and will create the need for substantial assistance. (This will affect Russians now living in the peripheries just as much as the nationals from these peripheries now residing in Russia.) Where should they go? Where will they find new housing? How will they get by until they have new employment? This must not become merely the personal problem of these individuals: it should be the concern of the above-mentioned panel of experts, supported by a system of government-sponsored compensations. And every newly formed state must provide explicit guarantees of minority rights.

More complex still will be the problem of devising a painless method of partitioning the national economies or the establishment of trade links and industrial cooperation on an independent basis.

Only in the course of implementing this work, or perhaps only after it is completed, will every national entity come to recognize its genuine problems, rather than that chronic "nationality problem" which has chafed our necks to the point where it has distorted all our feelings and our sense of reality.

Some jarring surprises from that future are already revealing themselves to us. How impatiently Georgia has been yearning for independence! (One notes in this connection that Russia had not conquered Georgia militarily; Lenin did that in 1921.) But look what is already happening: oppression of the Abkhazians, oppression of the Ossetians, and the Meskhetian Turks exiled from Georgia by Stalin are being refused the right to return to the land of their birth.[18] Can this really be what long-desired national freedom is all about?

Whatever we undertake, whatever aspect of contemporary political life we choose to reflect upon, none of us can expect any positive results as long as our cruel will pursues only our *self-interest,* overlooking even the humblest kind of morality, to say nothing of absolute justice.

URGENT MEASURES FOR THE RUSSIAN UNION

After three-quarters of a century we have all grown so poor, so tainted, and so filled with despair, that many of us are ready to give up, and it seems that the intercession of heaven alone can save us.

But miracles do not descend upon those who make no effort on their own behalf.

The fate of our children, our will to live, our millennial history, and the spirit of our ancestors, which must surely have been transferred to us in some fashion—all these things together will help us find the strength to prevail.

We may have been granted no time for reflecting upon the best-suited paths of development, no time to put together a reasoned program, and we may have no choice other than racing around frantically, plugging leaks, while imperative demands close in upon us, each one clamoring for priority. Yet we must preserve presence of mind and the wisdom of circumspection in our choice of initial measures.

I cannot presume to enumerate all these steps by myself; this must be done by a council drawing on the clearest practical minds and the best available energies. All things cry out for help in our present-day economy, and we simply cannot go on without pointing them in the right direction. Our people must urgently be made aware of the meaning of work, after half a century when no one could see any advantage to putting forth an effort—which is why nobody is available to raise crops or tend the cattle. Millions are inhabiting spaces that cannot be called homes, or are forced to spend decades in filthy dormitories. Dire poverty stalks the elderly and the handicapped. Our once magnificent expanses are befouled by industrial dumps and scarred by vehicle tracks due to the lack of roads. Nature, disdained so ungratefully by us, is taking its revenge, and the radioactive blotches from Chernobyl and elsewhere are spreading ominously.

On top of all this, must we now prepare to resettle those compatriots who are losing their places of residence? Yes, unavoidably so.

Wherever shall we find the money?

But, then, how long shall we continue supplying and propping up the tyrannical regimes we have implanted the world over, regimes which are incapable of supporting themselves and which are nothing if not insatiable squanderers of our wealth: Cuba, Vietnam, Ethiopia,

Angola, North Korea. We mind everyone's business, after all, and the above list is far from complete, with thousands of our "advisers" roaming about in all sorts of unlikely places. And after all the blood spilled in Afghanistan, isn't it a shame to let that country go? So, should we not dole out money there as well? . . . All this adds up to tens of billions each year.

He who cuts off *all this* at one fell stroke will deserve to be called a patriot and a true statesman.

How long and for what purpose must we keep producing ever more types of offensive weapons? And why the naval presence in all the world's oceans? Do we wish to seize the planet? The cost of all this escalates to hundreds of billions yearly. This, too, must be cut off without delay. The space program can also wait.

There is, furthermore, the preferential supplying of Eastern Europe with our ever-exploited raw materials. But we've had our stint of living together as a "socialist camp," and enough is enough. We rejoice for the countries of Eastern Europe, may they thrive in freedom, but let them pay for everything at world prices.

But what if this is not enough? Then we must stop reckless capital investment in industries that do not show signs of recovery.

There are, finally, the unimaginably huge assets of the Communist Party, a topic of much recent discussion.

They certainly did manage to appropriate a lot of goods from the population over seventy years, and to use it for their pleasure. Of course, there is no way to get back all that has been wasted, scattered, and plundered, but let them at least return what is left: the buildings, resorts, special farms, and publishing houses. And let them fund their operations with income derived from membership fees. (And for service on specifically Party posts, it is the Party, not the state, that should pay pension benefits.)

And the whole army of appointive bureaucrats, that parasitic multimillion-strong governing apparatus which inhibits all living forces in the nation—with their high salaries, various benefits, and special stores—we shall feed no more! Let them earn what they can by engaging in useful labor. Under the new order, eighty percent of the ministries and committees will also become unnecessary.

So that the money will come from all these sources.

And what have five or six years of the much-heralded "perestroika" been used for? For some pathetic reshuffling within the Central Committee. For the slapping together of an ugly and artificial electoral system designed to allow the Party to continue clinging to power. For the promulgation of flawed, confusing, and indecisive laws.

No, it is clear that the path to resolving even the most

urgent issues will not become open to us, nor shall we be able to attain anything really useful, until the Communist Party of Lenin will do more than yield on one constitutional provision:[19] it must remove itself completely from all involvement in the economy and affairs of state; it must cease controlling us, even where this entails only a particular aspect of our life or a specific locality. One would prefer to see this happen without the Party's being squeezed out or ejected by force, but rather as a result of its own public repentance: an acknowledgment by the Party that it has led the country into an abyss by a long series of crimes, cruelties, and absurdities, and that it does not know the way out. That's what would be timely now, not the current attempt to fashion a new Russian Communist Party for the sake of an odious continuity,[20] one that passes all the blood and filth onto the name of Russia and plods against the tide of history. A public admission by the Party of its guilt, its crimes, and its helplessness would at least be the first step toward alleviating the oppressiveness of our moral atmosphere.

And above us there still towers the concrete monolith of the KGB, also blocking our movement into the future. The assertion that they are particularly needed now for international intelligence-gathering is but a transparent stratagem; it is obvious that the reverse is true. Their only goal is to survive for their own sake and to suppress all movement among the people. Given its seventy-year record of bloodstained villainy, this Cheka-KGB can no longer have either justification or right to exist.

LAND

There must have been a reason why the earth was given the miraculous and blessed property of bearing fruit. And those conglomerations of people who are incapable of availing themselves of this property are surely lost.

Land embodies moral as well as economic values for human beings, a point persuasively argued in the writings of Gleb Uspensky, Dostoevsky, and others.

A weakening desire to work the land is a great danger to the national character. Among our people, the peasant sensibility has been trod underfoot and expunged so thoroughly that it may be too late, far too late, for it to be revived.

The manner in which the leasing of land [*arenda*] is being introduced today is largely an exercise in deceit and mockery, it makes little sense, and it will only kill off the desire in those who are reaching out to the land. At present, lessees are placed in suffocating dependency to the collective farm or state farm authorities, who can ignore the law at will; poor quality, abandoned lands are frequently allocated for leasing; the charges are set at inflated levels along with the cost of implements, while the lessee is forced to turn over his produce at a discount; the feed promised for delivery may not materialize or the animals taken on for fattening may be confiscated, wiping out large investments in money and effort; the agricultural-equipment firm can suddenly renege on a contract. And, in any case, a piece of land does not by itself mean freedom for the peasant: he also needs a free market, access to transportation, financial credit, technical repair facilities, and construction materials.

We embark on all reforms in the worst of all possible ways, and this is a case in point. The only thing accomplished has been harm to the cause, and people are being deprived of what little faith they had left in the promises of the regime.

Compared to the collective farm system, the personal leasing of land from a local self-governing body (not a collective farm) is unquestionably a step in the direction of improving our agriculture. Within the limits set up for a given region (as determined by a systematic land assessment), leasing should be for life, with the unrestricted right to pass the parcel of land to one's heirs; dispossession must not occur due to illness in the lessee's family, but only in cases of negligent land use; the lessee must have the right to give up his holdings, in which case he should be reimbursed for any investment he has made in the land or in buildings he has erected. (No special administrative mechanism needs to be set up for this purpose, since the instances enumerated above will not be numerous, and could be handled by the local *zemstvo*.)

But because we have gotten out of the habit of working the land, and also due to the justified distrust of the authorities, who have cheated us all too often, it may well be that leasing will no longer be attractive to the populace. What is more, the leasing option will not be economically competitive with private ownership of land, which guarantees the long-term improvement of the plot rather than its depletion, and which alone can ensure that our agriculture will not continue to lag behind the West. When we anticipate and demand initiative in all spheres of life, how can we prohibit it with respect to land? To deny private ownership of land to the village is to finish it off forever.

At the same time, private ownership must be introduced cautiously. In Stolypin's time,[21] there was already a strict requirement that land must pass to actual peasant farmers, not to major speculators or to surrogates through joint-stock companies. Today there is nothing left of our eradicated peasantry; the anonymous speculators of our "shadow economy" have gained in freewheeling adroitness and have accumulated their initial capital; and our graft-ridden administration is incapable of close oversight. The result is that today those very "joint-stock companies," "organizations," and "cooperatives" could well buy up huge tracts of land in order to lease them out on their own. (This is not to mention the acquisition of land by foreigners.) Such purchases must clearly be prohibited. If the land were to end up in the hands of major proprietors, the lives of everyone else would be noticeably hemmed in. (Nor can we permit this, in view of the imminent overpopulation of our planet, and obviously of our country as well.)

Purchases of land must benefit from a multi-year repayment plan, as well as preferential tax treatment. Any limitation imposed on the size of lot available for purchase in a given area would not in itself affect the quality of work negatively or restrict freedom. On the contrary, the efforts of every owner would be directed not at expanding his possessions but at improving yield and raising efficiency. The fact that tiny private plots [*priusadebnye uchastki*] have fed the country under the vaunted collective farm system demonstrates that our people can work miracles along these lines, even under the most difficult and hostile conditions imposed by the regime.

Restricting the acreage of purchases would leave reserves of land that could be distributed in small plots to workers who might wish to raise their own vegetable crop, or to city dwellers who seek relief from their cooped-up existence. This distribution should be free, with cultivation of the land the only requirement, and an area equal in size to this plot should be included as a free portion of the land purchased by farmers.

There should be enough land for everybody.

THE ECONOMY

Stolypin believed that it is impossible to create a state governed by laws without first having an independent citizen: social structure precedes any political program and is a more fundamental entity.

But there can be no independent citizen without private property.

After seventy years of propaganda, our brains have been instilled with the notion that one must fear private property and avoid hired labor as though they were the work of the devil: that represents a major victory of ideology over our human essence. (Our entire view of Western economy has been likewise inculcated in a form that is a caricature of reality.)

The truth is that ownership of modest amounts of property which does not oppress others must be seen as an integral component of personality, and as a factor contributing to its stability, while conscientiously performed, fairly compensated hired labor is a form of mutual assistance and a source of goodwill among people.

Why should we continue to cling to the centralized, ineffective, and ideologically regulated economic system that has reduced the whole country to poverty? Can it be just in order to maintain the parasitic bureaucracy that would otherwise lose its last reason for being?

Of course, we must take every measure to soften the blow that will be dealt to millions of unprepared and unadapted people by the transition to a market economy. Fortunately (or unfortunately!), our country now has budgetary outlays of billions upon billions that are being squandered in ways enumerated earlier: we can turn to this source.

Six years will soon have passed, but the clamorous perestroika has yet to have any healing effect on either agriculture or industry. It is a delay that represents years in the people's life given up to pointless suffering.

But any thoughtless wholesale adoption of a foreign type of economy (economies that have taken shape gradually over centuries) would also have ruinous consequences. I have no special expertise in economics, and I have no wish to venture definitive proposals here. What specific procedures make possible the transition from the state ownership of enterprises to private or cooperatively held ownership; what financial conditions must be provided for this purpose; what part of the assets currently held by the state—such items as the transportation system, the merchant fleet, the timberlands, water and land resources, and mineral wealth—will remain under state control and to what degree they should be ceded to local authorities; which budget will provide for social security, education, and housing construction; what new labor legislation will need to be enacted—all these questions have already been the subject of detailed studies by economists, who, admittedly, disagree strongly among themselves.

But the overall picture seems clear enough: healthy private initiative must be given wide latitude, and small enterprises of every type must be encouraged and protected, since they are what will ensure the most rapid flowering of every locality. At the same time there should be firm legal limits to the unchecked concentration of capital; no monopolies should be permitted to form in any sector, and no enterprise should be in control of any other. The creation of monopolies brings with it the risk of deteriorating quality: a firm can permit itself to turn out goods that are not durable, in order to sustain demand. For centuries, both manufacturers and owners took pride in the durability of their merchandise, but today (in the West) we see a numbing sequence of new, ever new and flashy models, while the healthy notion of *repair* is disappearing: items that are just barely damaged must be discarded and replaced by new ones, an act inimical to the human sense of self-limitation, and a wasteful extravagance.

To this, one must add the psychological plague of inflation in the developed countries: as labor productivity grows, prices do not fall—they rise! This is not progress but an all-consuming economic fire. (Prices went unchanged for a century at a time in the Russia of old.)

The pressures of ownership and profit-taking must not be allowed to reach a level where this becomes a social evil that is destructive of the health of society. Excessive growth in any sector of the economy must be regulated by means of antitrust laws and progressive taxation. Banks are necessary as the operational centers of financial activity, but they must not be permitted to become usurious growths and the hidden masters of all life.

It likewise seems clear that the price of withdrawing from communism should not be an inequitable sell-off of our mineral resources, our land, and especially our forests to foreign capitalists. It is a dangerous idea to attempt to salvage by means of foreign capital what has been destroyed by our internal disarray. Investments will flow into our country whenever high margins of profit will be anticipated. But Western capital must not be lured in on terms that are advantageous to it but humiliating to us, in come-and-rule-over-us style. There would be no rectifying this later, and we would turn into a colony. (But, then, it is also true that in the three-quarters of a century of Soviet rule we have indeed sunk to the level of a colony; there is no other word for it.) Foreign investment must be permitted on the strict condition that the economic stimulation it introduces will be exceeded neither by the profits exported nor by the damage to the natural environment. These conditions will also spur our native industry to approach the qualitative level of developed countries.

It cannot be that the work habits of our people have been completely suppressed and forgotten. We have seen the Japanese recover from their disaster and even gain ascendancy by virtue of their superior work ethic, not through any foreign infusions. And as soon as the heavy hand of the state ceases constricting our every movement, and remuneration reaches equitable levels, the quality of work will improve at once, and skilled craftsmen will come to light everywhere. And although we may not soon reach the stage where our products have an appeal on the international market, it is also true that for a country of our size and wealth it is possible to manage with the domestic market alone for a considerable time.

But, obviously, no normal economic life is compatible with our current slave-like and police-enforced "residence permit" system.

We must learn to respect healthy, honest, and intelligent private commerce (and to distinguish it from predatory dealings built on bribes or the swindling of inept management): such commerce stimulates and unifies society, and it is one of the very first things we need.

I shall not venture to make suggestions on matters related to monetary, budgetary, or tax policies. But it is clear that in addition to strict environmental controls, and substantial fines for despoiling the environment, financial incentives should be in place for efforts aimed at restoring or protecting nature, as well as at bringing back traditional crafts.

THE PROVINCES

It decidedly does not depend on Moscow, Petrograd, Kiev, and Minsk whether our country will flourish economically; that depends on the provinces. The key to the viability of the country and the vitality of its culture lies in liberating the provinces from the pressure of the capitals and at the same time freeing those unhealthy giants of the unnatural way in which they have become overburdened by their size and the multitude of their functions—factors that deprive them of a normal life. Nor do the capitals possess the moral grounds for seeing the rebirth of the country in terms of their own needs, not after six decades during which the provinces had been abandoned to hunger, humiliation, and insignificance.

All our provincial districts, all the expanses of the Russian Union must acquire complete freedom in economic and cultural terms, together with strong (and increasingly influential) local self-government. Our country will not be able to lead a full and independent life unless there emerge perhaps forty centers of vitality and illumination throughout the breadth of the land. Each would be a focus of economic activity as well as of culture, education, library resources, and publishing enterprises, so that the population of the surrounding area could receive a full share of cultural sustenance, while the younger generation could count on the availability of educational and other facilities that would not be inferior to those in the capital. Only in such circumstances can the development of a large country proceed in a balanced manner.

The unique local features of a given region will come back to life around each of such forty cities. And only this kind of dispersion will bring about the repair of the ruined local system and promote the construction of new roads, towns, and villages.

This process will be particularly important in the vastness of Greater Siberia, a land we have been crippling—blindly and mindlessly—ever since the first Five-Year Plan,[22] instead of promoting its prosperous development.

In this, as in so much else, the road back to health must begin at the grass roots.

FAMILY AND SCHOOL

Although everything linked to the ruin of today must be tended to without delay, it is even more urgent to lay the foundation of that which takes shape slowly: in the years when we will be trying to make up for lost time in every sphere, what kind of development will take place in our children? This concerns areas from pediatric medicine and early childhood care to education. For if this is not remedied immediately, we shall have no future to talk about.

The disastrous plight of women in our country is common knowledge and a regular topic of conversation that evokes no arguments, since everything is clear. The same is true of the falling birthrate, infant mortality and morbidity, and the terrifying state of our maternity clinics, day-care centers, and kindergartens.

Normal families have virtually ceased to exist in our country. Yet family ills are at the same time critically serious maladies for the state, and the family has a fundamental role in the salvation of our future. Women must have the opportunity to return to their families to take care of the children; the salary earned by men must make this possible. (However, given the expected high unemployment of the initial period, this goal will not be attainable right away: some families will be glad that at least the woman will have kept her job.)

The schools are an equally urgent concern of ours. To think of the number of foolish experiments to which we subjected the schools in the course of seventy years! Yet only rarely did the schools produce knowledgeable individuals, and then only in some subjects, and only in select institutions of some large cities. A provincial Lomonosov,[23] to say nothing of one coming from a village, would today have no chance of emerging or of fighting his way through (to begin with, he would have been stopped by the regulation on residence permits). The quality of the schools must be raised not only in the elite institutions of the capitals; by persistent effort this movement must start at the lowest levels and encompass the entire country. This task is in no sense less urgent than all our economic ones. Our schools have long provided poor training and inadequate education. It is intolerable that the general guidance of students should be viewed as an essentially unpaid extra burden placed on teachers: it must be compensated by a reduction of the individual's teaching load. And all of today's curricula and textbooks in the humanities are destined for fundamental revision if not outright rejection. And the drumming-in of atheism must be stopped immediately.

The truth is that we must begin not with schoolchildren but with the teachers, for we have pushed them below the subsistence level and into poverty; the men who could leave the profession for better-paying jobs have done so. But schoolteachers are supposed to be the cream of the nation, they are people with a calling, to whom we entrust our future. (Where did we train the teachers of today and what ideological gibberish did they have to assimilate? All changes and all efforts to salvage true knowledge must begin with revamping the curricula at the teachers' colleges.)

In the near future we can probably also expect to see the appearance of tuition-charging private schools which will surpass the standards of the school system in particular subjects or in some other specific educational aspects. But such schools must not institute irresponsibly arbitrary curricula; they should be under the supervision and control of local educational authorities.

Unprovided for by either family or school, our young people have been developing in the direction of unreflecting and barbarous emulation of things enticingly foreign, not to say in the direction of crime. The Iron Curtain of yesterday gave our country superb protection against all the positive features of the West: against the West's civil liberties, its respect for the individual, its freedom of personal activity, its high level of general welfare, its spontaneous charitable movements. But the Curtain did not reach all the way to the bottom, permitting the continuous seepage of liquid manure—the self-indulgent and squalid "popular mass culture," the utterly vulgar fashions, and the byproducts of immoderate publicity—all of which our deprived young people have greedily absorbed. Western youth run wild from a feeling of surfeit, while ours mindlessly ape these antics despite their poverty. And today's television obligingly distributes these streams of filth throughout the land. (To object to any of this is considered a sign of hopeless conservatism. But it is instructive to note the voices of alarm that have been raised in Israel about a similar phenomenon: "The Hebrew cultural revolution did not take place in order to make our country capitulate to American cultural imperialism and its byproducts . . . Western intellectual trash.")

It is no longer news and has been repeatedly addressed in print that our library resources are in physical danger, that our reading rooms are half empty, and that our museums are suffering from neglect. All these entities are in need of state assistance, since they cannot subsist on ticket sales in the manner of theaters, movie houses, and art exhibits. (But sports should certainly not be financed by the state, even in the hope of gaining world fame: let the collection of funds be purely voluntary, while basic physical and athletic training is provided in the schools.)

IS THE SYSTEM OF GOVERNMENT REALLY THE CENTRAL ISSUE?

There is no escaping the fact that our country has cruelly forfeited the entire twentieth century: all our much-trumpeted achievements have turned out to be illusory. From a flourishing condition we have been hurled back to a state of semi-barbarity, and we are sitting amid the wreckage.

We hold passionate discussions about the kind of government system that would suit us, and the kind that would not, since this, we claim, is the key to everything. And we argue about what trendy new party or "front" can now lead us on to success.

Yet recovery is today not a matter of simply identifying the most convenient system of government and then hastily cobbling together a marvelous constitution, article by article. We must demonstrate better foresight than did our luckless fathers and grandfathers in 1917, so that we might not repeat the chaos of that February by putting ourselves at the mercy of tempting slogans and breathless orators, or otherwise reproducing the self-chosen path to a shameful conclusion.[24]

A decisive change in regime calls for thoughtfulness and a sense of responsibility. Not every newfangled idea necessarily yields beneficial results. Our incomparable critics of the government in 1916[25] turned out to be entirely unprepared for the power they gained a few months later, in 1917, and managed to ruin everything. There is no guarantee whatever that the new leaders now coming to the fore will immediately prove to be farsighted and sober-minded. Thus, a critic of the despised "System" (as he termed it with appropriate caution), his electoral victory barely behind him, demonstrated a lack of sensitivity toward the land that sustains the capital. For sixty years Moscow has been fed at the expense of the hungry countryside, having tacitly agreed since the early thirties to a deal whereby it would share benefits with the authorities. Moscow thus became something of a privileged island, with material and cultural conditions different from those in the rest of the country. And that has altered the psychology of that part of the Muscovite public which has the opportunity to speak out, but which for decades has not expressed the true pain of the land.

Amid the tumult of mass meetings and of multiplying splinter parties, we have failed to notice that we have donned the gaudy circus attire of February—of those ill-fated eight months in 1917. And the few observers who did take note of the similarity are gushing with blind elation about "the new February Revolution." (To make the analogy complete, the black banners of anarchy have also made their appearance.)

After a cannibalistic period lasting three-quarters of a century, after the exorbitant price we have already paid, and given the fact that in terms of the political spectrum we happen to have ended up on the side with a tradition of strong central authority, it behooves us not to make rash moves toward chaos. For, as 1917 has taught us, anarchy is the ultimate peril.

Unless one craves revolution, a state must possess the qualities of continuity and stability. In this sense, the new statute creating a potentially strong presidency will prove useful for many years to come. Given our massive backlog of afflictions, further complicated by the inevitable separation of the peripheral republics, it is simply not feasible for us to attempt to resolve issues of government structure at the same time as we address problems relating to land, food, housing, private property, finances, and the army. Some elements of the current structure will have to serve for the time being, for the simple reason that they already exist.

It goes without saying that we shall gradually reshape the entire state organism. This undertaking must begin somewhere in the "periphery"; it should not be tackled all at once. What is clear is that the process should start at the local level with grass-roots issues. While preserving a strong central authority, we must patiently and persistently expand the rights of local communities.

With time, we shall of course adopt some particular type of political structure, but in view of our total inexperience in such matters, our choice may not be a felicitous one at first, not something suited to the specific needs of our country. We must resolutely seek our own path here. We have lately been assuring ourselves that there is no need of any quest or reflection on our part, that it is simply a matter of adopting "the way it is done in the West" as quickly as possible.

But in the West it is done in, oh, so many different ways, with every country following its own tradition.

One might think that we are the only people who need neither look back nor pay heed to the wise things said in our country before we were born.

Or we can put it this way: the structure of the state is secondary to the spirit of human relations. Given human integrity, any honest system is acceptable, but given human rancor and selfishness, even the most sweeping of democracies would become unbearable. If the people themselves lack fairness and honesty, this will come to the surface under any system.

Political activity is by no means the principal mode of human life, and politics is hardly the most sought-after enterprise for the majority of the people. The more energetic the political activity in a country, the greater is the loss to spiritual life. Politics must not swallow up all of a people's spiritual and creative energies. Beyond upholding its *rights*, mankind must defend its soul, freeing it for reflection and feeling.

TAKING OUR OWN MEASURE

The strength or weakness of a society depends more on the level of its spiritual life than on its level of industrialization. Neither a market economy nor even general abundance constitutes the crowning achievement of human life. The purity of social relations is a more fundamental value than the level of abundance. If a nation's spiritual energies have been exhausted, it will not be saved from collapse by the most perfect government structure or by any industrial development: a tree with a rotten core cannot stand. This is so because, of all the possible freedoms, the one that will inevitably come to the fore will be the freedom to be unscrupulous: that is the freedom that can be neither prevented nor anticipated by any law. It is an unfortunate fact that a pure social atmosphere cannot be legislated into being.

And that is why the destruction of our souls over three-quarters of a century is the most terrifying thing of all.

It is terrible to see that the corrupt ruling class—the multimillion-strong appointed bureaucracy [*nomenklatura*] which serves Party and state—is incapable of voluntarily giving up any of the privileges it has appropriated to itself. For decades this class has lived shamelessly at the expense of the people, and it would like to continue doing so.

And have any of the former killers and persecutors been so much as forced from their jobs or deprived of their undeservedly ample pensions? We doted on Molotov until the day he died, we are still pampering Kaganovich and who knows how many unnamed others.[26] In Germany all such individuals, including far less important ones, were put on trial, but in our country it is *they* who are threatening us with lawsuits, while some, like the murderous Chekist Berzin, are even having monuments erected in their honor.[27] But it seems beyond us to punish state criminals, and we won't live to hear a word of repentance from any of them. Might they at least be subjected to a public moral trial? But no, it looks as if we'll have to crawl on as is . . .

And what about those glorious forces of glasnost and perestroika? Among these fashionable words we look in vain for the concept of *purification*. What we see is a stampede toward the new glasnost of all those tainted voices which had given decades of loyal service to totalitarianism. Of every four troubadours of today's glasnost, three are former toadies of Brezhnevism, and who among them has uttered a word of *personal* repentance instead of cursing the faceless "period of stagnation"?[28] And the same individuals who for decades have befuddled the minds of university students continue to hold forth self-confidently from the rostrums of our humanities departments. Tens of thousands of "smatterers" [*obrazovantsy*][29] in our country are tarnished by their hypocrisy and weather-vane mentality: should we not expect repentance from any of them, and must we really drag along these festering moral sores into our future?

And what about the soul-corroding practice of brutal

hazing [*dedovshchina*][30] in the military barracks to which our sons are subjected? Will this experience ever be erased from their minds?

And the pervasive animosity of our people toward one another? Just like that, for no reason. Anger at people who are completely blameless.

And should we really be surprised at the upsurge of criminal behavior among those whose access to all honest paths of development has been blocked throughout their young lives?

In the old days, Russian merchants had their "merchant's word" (for consummating transactions without a written contract), they had Christian beliefs, and engaged in large-scale charitable enterprises noted by history. Shall we live to see anything of the kind from the sharks bred in the murky waters of the Soviet underground?

West Germany was suffused with the feeling of repentance before the coming of their economic boom. But in our country no one has even begun to repent. And our glasnost is bedecked, festooned with the same old plump and heavy clusters of lies. Only we seem not to notice.

That is a recipe for warped development.

One would have liked to be encouraged by the positive potential of the Church. But alas, even today, when

everything in the country has begun to move, the stir-
rings of courage have had little impact on the Orthodox
hierarchy. (And at a time of general hardship, it is simply
imperative to renounce the attributes of wealth, so
temptingly offered by the regime.) The Church will become helpful to our social recovery only when it finds
the strength to free itself completely from the yoke of
the state and to restore a living bond with the people, a
bond so vividly clear even in the heyday of 1917, at the
time of the election of Metropolitans Tikhon and Veniamin, and the convocation of the Church Council.[31] If only
it were possible, in keeping with Christ's commandment, to manifest an example of fearlessness once
again, not only vis-à-vis the state: society, the burning
issues of today, and the Church itself must also be
openly addressed. The movement toward rebirth in this
sphere, as in all others, can be expected to com-
mence—it is already doing so—at the most humble levels, with the activity of rank-and-file clergymen, of par-
ishes united by a common purpose, and of selfless
parishioners.

SELF-LIMITATION

"Human rights" is currently the most fashionable and
most eagerly repeated slogan among us. (But we all

have very different things in mind. The educated class in capital cities visualizes human rights in terms of freedom of speech, of the press, of public assembly, and of emigration, but many would angrily demand curtailing the "rights" as they are seen by the ordinary people: the right to live and work in the same place where there is something to buy—which would bring millions into the capitals.)

"Human rights" are a fine thing, but how can we ourselves make sure that our rights do not expand at the expense of the rights of others? A society with unlimited rights is incapable of standing up to adversity. If we do not wish to be ruled by a coercive authority, then each of us must rein himself in. No constitutions, laws, or elections will by themselves assure equilibrium in a society, because it is human to persist in the pursuit of one's interests. Most people in a position to enhance their rights and seize more will do precisely that. (Hence the demise of all the ruling classes throughout history.) A stable society is achieved not by balancing opposing forces but by conscious self-limitation: by the principle that we are always duty-bound to defer to the sense of moral justice.

Only self-limitation will make possible the continued survival of the ever-proliferating and ever more tightly packed human race. The long process of human development will have been for nought if mankind does not become imbued with the spirit of self-limitation, for the freedom to seize and gorge oneself is something even animals possess. Human freedom, in contrast, includes voluntary self-limitation for the sake of others. Our duty must always exceed the freedom we have been granted.

May we succeed in assimilating this spirit, and, more important, in passing it on to our children. Self-limitation is above all necessary for the individual himself, for a sense of balance and tranquillity in his soul.

The inner opportunities here are many. Thus, after our long period of enforced ignorance, the hunger we feel is only natural: we avidly want to learn the truth about what happened to us. But some will already have noticed, others will do so shortly, that above and beyond this there flows an unendurable stream of information, much of it excessive and trivial, diminishing our soul and reaching a point where we must protect ourselves from it. Newspapers proliferate in today's world, each of them keeps swelling, and all vie with each other in their effort to overload us with information. There are ever more television channels, during the day as well as in the evening (Icelanders, in contrast, give up television entirely for at least a day each week); there is ever more clamor of a propagandistic, commercial, and diversionary nature (and to this day our country has to put up with the unceasing blare of loudspeakers over its open spaces). How can we protect the *right* of our ears to silence, and the right of our eyes to inner vision?

For our country to find a steady way out of its era of misfortunes—a goal which Russia may or may not attain—will be a task harder than shaking off the Tartar Yoke: the very backbone of the nation was not shattered at that time, and the people's Christian faith was not undermined.

In 1754, during the reign of the Empress Elizabeth, Pyotr Ivanovich Shuvalov came forward with a proposal bearing an astonishing title: *A Plan for Saving the People.*

An eccentric, no doubt?

But, then, such a formulation reflects the essence of state wisdom.

LOOKING

AHEAD

It won't do to hope that our current "time of troubles" will be followed by some kind of tranquil period with ample opportunity "to sit down and think over" our plans for the future. History is a continuum, and no one will grant us the favor of any breathing spell, just as the Russian Constituent Assembly was never given the chance "to sit down and think things over."[32] So that, no matter how painfully the burning issues of today weigh down upon us, it behooves us to give advance thought to the shape of our future arrangement. (And, in my own case, considerations of age make it uncertain whether I would be able to participate in the discussion of these issues.)

Before the Revolution, the bulk of our people had no experience with political concepts, and the ideas that were pounded into our heads by propaganda in the subsequent seventy years served only to cloud our minds. But now that our country has begun moving in the direction of real political life, and when the forms of the government-to-be are already being discussed, it is useful to focus on the precise meaning of some terms in order to prevent possible mistakes.

CONCERNING THE FORMS OF GOVERNMENT

Spengler correctly pointed out that the very concept of the state is differently understood in different cultures and that there is no definitive "best" form of government which needs to be borrowed from one great culture for use in another. And Montesquieu believed that there exists a particular form of government appropriate to every physical size of state, and that this form cannot simply be transposed to another state unless there is a match in physical dimensions.

For a given people, with its specific geography, history, traditions, and psychological makeup, the task is to set in place a structure that will lead to a flourishing of this people rather than to its decline and degeneration.

The state structure must necessarily take national traditions into account: "Stand in the crossroads and look, ask for the ancient paths: which is the good way? Take it and you will find rest for yourself" (Jeremiah 6:16).

A people has the unquestioned right to power, but its desire is not for power (such an ambition is characteristic of no more than perhaps two percent): above all, it seeks to have stable order. After witnessing the events of 1917, even the Christian socialist George Fedotov insisted on the need for a strong executive, going so far as to write that the executive should not depend closely on the legislative council, answering to it only at considerable intervals. (That seems pretty extreme.)

If one is to opt for the plan—set forth below—of building the institutions of freedom from the bottom up while temporarily preserving the existing formal features of the central authority, that process will take a number of years, and there will be time for substantial discussion of sound principles of state-building.

One can today make only tentative pronouncements about the future: we must leave maneuvering space to take into account our unfolding experience and any further thoughts on the matter. The ultimate form of government (if indeed there can be such a thing) will be the product of successive approximations and trials.

. . .

Plato, and Aristotle after him, identified three types of states. In the usual sequence these are: monarchy, or the rule of one; aristocracy, or the rule of the best or for the best purpose; and polity, or the rule of the people in a small city-state for the common good (we now term this democracy). The Greek writers went on to warn about the specific perversions of these categories into, respectively, tyranny, oligarchy, and mob rule.

Each of the three basic forms of rule can be beneficial if directed toward the public good, and all three become perverted when they serve private interests.

It would appear that since that time no one has created any structure that did not fit into these categories; the only additions were various types of constitutions. So that, if we disregard the complete absence of rule (i.e., anarchy, or the rule of every strong individual over every weak one), and avoid falling once more into the trap of totalitarianism, that twentieth-century invention, then we cannot be said to have much of a choice: the whole flow of modern history will unquestionably predispose us to choose democracy.

But in opting for democracy we must understand clearly just what we are choosing, what price we shall have to pay, and that we are choosing it as a means, not as an end in itself. The contemporary philosopher Karl Popper has said that one chooses democracy, not because it abounds in virtues, but only in order to avoid tyranny. We choose it in full awareness of its faults and with the intention of seeking ways to overcome them.

Many new countries have in recent years suffered a fiasco just after introducing democracy; yet, despite such evidence, this same period has seen an elevation of democracy from a particular state structure into a sort of universal principle of human existence, almost a cult.

We shall nevertheless attempt to clarify the meaning of this term.

WHAT DEMOCRACY IS AND WHAT IT IS NOT

Tocqueville viewed the concepts of democracy and liberty as polar opposites. He was an ardent proponent of liberty, but not at all of democracy. For John Stuart Mill, unlimited democracy held the danger of "the tyranny of the majority," a situation that, from the point of view of an individual, is indistinguishable from the tyranny of one.

George Fedotov believed that democracy had been distorted by the dehumanizing assault of nineteenth-century atheistic materialism. And the twentieth-century Austrian statesman Joseph Schumpeter referred to democracy as the surrogate faith of intellectuals deprived of religion, cautioning against any view of democracy outside the context of time and place.

The Russian philosopher Sergei Levitsky has proposed distinguishing what he has called the *essence* of democracy, consisting of (1) individual freedom and (2) a government of laws, from its secondary, non-mandatory features, namely (1) the parliamentary system or (2) universal suffrage, neither of which he considered self-evident.

Respect for the individual represents a broader principle than democracy and it is a principle that must be ensured without fail. But this need not necessarily be rendered only by means of a parliamentary system.

But it is also true that the rights of individuals must not be exalted to the point of eclipsing the rights of society. As Pope John Paul II stated in a 1981 speech in the Philippines, when national security comes into conflict with human rights, the former must take priority, because without the integrity of the larger structure the life of individuals will crumble as well.

And President Ronald Reagan expressed his thoughts on democracy as follows in his 1988 remarks at Moscow University: Democracy is less a system of government than a means of *limiting* government, preventing it from interfering in the development of the true sources of human values that are found only in family and faith.

"Democracy" is today a supremely fashionable word in our country, mouthed in endless variations, flaunted, brandished, and exploited for personal advantage. But there is no tangible evidence that we have given close thought to the exact meaning of this term.

Following the bitter experience of 1917, when we plunged headlong into what we had thought was democracy, Vasili Maklakov, a prominent leader of the Constitutional Democrats, reminded us all of a simple truth by the following admission: "In order to function, democracy needs a certain level of political discipline among the populace." But this is precisely what we lacked in 1917, and one fears that there is even less of it today.

UNIVERSAL AND EQUAL SUFFRAGE, DIRECT ELECTIONS, SECRET BALLOTS

When Stalin introduced our travesty of an election system in 1937, even he felt the need to give it the outward trappings of universal and equal suffrage, direct vote, and secret ballot; i.e., the pattern that the contemporary world looks upon almost as if it were an indisputable law of nature. But after the French Revolution (as reflected in the Constitution of 1791) elections were not yet conducted in this fashion, with various restrictions and inequalities affecting the franchise. The concept of universal suffrage prevailed in France only after the Revolution of 1848. And in England throughout the nineteenth century distinguished proponents of "constitutional order" fought for a system which would guarantee that no majority could ever tyrannize a minority and that there would be representation in parliament of each stratum of society that enjoyed respect and was aware of its responsibilities for the fate of the nation. This was an effort to preserve the foundations upon which the country had developed. But, after 1918, England, too, gravitated toward universal suffrage.

Dostoevsky pronounced the idea of universal and equal suffrage "the most absurd invention of the nineteenth century." At any rate, it is not Newton's Law, and it is permissible to have doubts about its alleged merits. Does not "universal and equal" clash with the tremendous inequality among individuals in terms of their talents, their contribution to society, their ages, their life experience, their degree of rootedness in the country and in the locality? It represents the triumph of bare quantity over substance and quality. What is more, such elections assume that the nation lacks all structure: that it is not a living organism but a mere mechanical conglomeration of disparate individuals. Nor does secret voting represent something to be admired in and of itself. It facilitates insincerity or is an unfortunate necessity born of fear. There are still places in the world where voting is conducted openly.

Direct elections—i.e., those in which deputies of all levels are elected directly by popular vote—are especially open to question in a country as huge as ours. Such a system results in voters not knowing their deputies, a situation that benefits the smoothest talkers as well as individuals with strong behind-the-scenes support.

Electoral systems and the various methods of tabulating votes were examined in elaborate detail by commissions and party committees in Russia during the spring and summer of 1917—which is why the Constituent Assembly was so lamentably late.[33] All the democratic parties of the time were opposed to four-tier, three-tier, and even two-tier elections because such a system provides for personal knowledge of the candidates at each stage in the process, with the elected representatives thus having closer links to their district and "home turf"—but thereby depriving the parties of the ability to impose their own candidates from the center. The head of the Constitutional Democratic Party, Pavel Milyukov, insisted that only *direct* elections in *large* electoral districts could "ensure the election of intelligent and politically trained representatives."

If that is what one needs.

ELECTORAL PROCEDURES

The aim of universal suffrage is to permit the Popular Will to be manifested: that genuine Will which is supposed to guide everything in a direction most advantageous to the people. Yet no one has been able to say whether such a single Will exists at all, or to define its qualities. And it is remarkable that different systems of counting votes will produce different or even diametrically opposed readings of this Popular Will.

Most of us today do not attach much importance to the actual mechanics of the voting system, but in fact this has a very substantial impact on the results.

At least three electoral systems vie with each other in today's world: proportional representation, plurality voting, and voting based on an absolute majority.

Elections under the system of proportional representation virtually always involve voting for slates or "tickets" of candidates, naturally drawn up by the party: in each district every party proposes its list of candidates (typically, for several seats at a time, this being more convenient in terms of party control and campaign efficiency). In the process, individual candidates are stripped of personal responsibility vis-à-vis the voter and made responsible to the party alone, while voters are deprived of the ability to pick a candidate they trust rather than a party. (One can distinguish two subdivisions within this system: when voters cannot alter the order of priority in a list of candidates, this being the prerogative of the party; and the alternative, when voters are free to choose candidates from a given slate or even to offer a slate of their own, something that admittedly makes the mechanics of vote tabulation very complicated. There exists a further variant where districts are divided into sections with only one candidate for each, but district committees then tally up votes by party anyway, allocating seats on a proportional basis to parties, not individuals. In every case the choice of specific individuals depends primarily on the party.)

In 1917 all political parties from the Constitutional Democrats to the Bolsheviks expressed a preference for the proportional representation system and for electoral districts with multiple candidates. This was strongly endorsed by the influential Constitutional Democrat Iosif Gessen, for instance, who argued that such an arrangement allowed for the greatest ease of party organization, whereas "under the system of electing individual candidates, the party can frequently lose its guiding influence." Similar approval was voiced by Vladimir Ulyanov, alias Lenin, who thought that the election of "party representatives, rather than individuals," was "one of the most progressive electoral procedures." Evidently he had good reason to hold the system in such high regard. Proportional representation based on party tickets grants inordinate power to those who compile lists of candidates, and gives an advantage to large and well-organized parties. There is the further specific benefit of being able to place the party's centrally located activists on the ballot in remote districts where these individuals do not reside, and thus to ensure their election. The party convention held by the Constitutional Democrats in the summer of 1917 put particular emphasis on freeing candidates from the requirement to reside in their election district. That, it was held, "gives the Central Committee the opportunity to conduct the election campaign in a centralized manner." All the other parties insisted on much the same thing. One might call this *centralized democracy.*

Proportional representation usually ensures that small minorities have some kind of voice in a representative assembly, but at the same time it leads to a multiplicity of parliamentary factions and a dissipation of energy on petty squabbles. Or it can tempt parties to improve their status by forming coalitions that cynically disregard their platforms for the sake of gaining votes and taking control of the government. The contemporary world offers striking examples of this type of weakness and of the protracted governmental crises associated with it.

The plurality voting system can also bring about unnatural compromises between parties, but in the form of pre-election alliances. Under this system, the party or bloc that is even slightly ahead of the others receives the lion's share of the seats, while those trailing even by a tiny margin can lose everything. Thus, it is possible to receive 49 percent of the popular vote without winning any parliamentary seats. And in the case of uneven distribution of electoral districts, the plurality system can bring victory to a minority, as happened in France, for instance, in 1893, 1898, and 1902, when several winning candidates collected fewer votes than the losers; in the two latter election years, 53 percent of the voters had no representation whatever in the Chamber of Deputies.

On the other hand, this system provides for a stable government.

The absolute majority electoral system which is being introduced in our country (and which permits runoff elections) also excludes the smaller parties but makes it possible to bargain for votes between the first and second round of voting.

Under a two-party system as in the United States, independent candidates have little weight and the vote is given to one of the two parties, both of which have powerful organizations and abundant financial support. In this system, social dissatisfaction takes considerable time to find an outlet and may not be able to do so in the course of a single election campaign, but when it does, it is articulated in negative terms: ejecting the party in power becomes the top priority, even when there is no certainty about the plans of those who will replace it.

Thus, the mere system of tallying votes can entail radical differences in the makeup of a government and of its program, which—naturally—manifests Popular Will.

. . .

But then it must be said that voting in general, whatever the method of tabulating the results, does not represent a quest for truth. Everything is reduced to numbers, to a simplistic mathematical concept, and to the absorption of a minority by the majority—always a risky process, since a minority is in no sense less important for society than a majority, and the latter can well stray into error. "You will not be led into wrong-doing by the majority nor, when giving evidence in a lawsuit, side with the majority to pervert the course of justice" (Exodus 23:2).

One should add that election campaigns involving large numbers of voters and conducted among an electorate with no direct knowledge of the candidates can be so frivolous and shrill that, given the frequent bias of the media, a large proportion of the voters can turn away in disgust. And television, though it may bring out a candidate's appearance as well as his public demeanor, does nothing to reveal his abilities as a statesman. Campaigns of this sort invariably entail the degradation of political thought. Talent and creativity are both essential for successful and beneficial leadership, but how is one to select these qualities through a universal vote conducted over a huge area? The system does not inspire political figures to rise above their political interests, and may in fact have the opposite effect: a campaign based on moral principles can become a recipe for defeat.

In his study of the United States in the nineteenth century, Tocqueville concluded that democracy denotes the reign of mediocrity (although extraordinary circumstances prevailing in a country can and do bring strong personalities to the fore).

REPRESENTING THE PEOPLE

Once a candidate is elected, he becomes a *representative of the people*.

Athenian democracy rejected the very idea of representation as a form of oligarchy. But, then, it could afford to do so, in view of the small territory in which it functioned.

The French Estates-General, on the other hand, immediately after convening in 1789 passed a law to the effect that every representative must henceforth be considered merely a part of that collective body which in fact *is* the will of the people. By this action, deputies were cut off from their voters and from any personal responsibilities toward them.

Our four consecutive State Dumas[34] were not a true reflection of the depth and breadth of Russia; they represented only certain narrow strata in a few cities, while the bulk of the population did not really focus its attention on the elections and parties of the time. And Vasili Maklakov, a brilliant Duma veteran, had to admit that "the will of the people" is a fiction even in a democracy: what is taken to stand for this entity is nothing more profound than a majority decision in parliament.

In any case, it is not feasible for the people to give their representatives precise instructions concerning all future contingencies. Nor is there a stimulus that will impel those deputies holding office to rise above their *future* electoral interests and above party machinations so as to serve only the clearly perceived interests of the country, even if (as is probably inevitable) such a stance should be detrimental to party interests or to the deputies themselves. As a result, the actions that are taken are those having immediate appeal to the voters, even though the long view might suggest that these actions will bring them harm. And in a country as large as ours, the possibility of keeping tabs on elected representatives is correspondingly reduced, while the chance of abuses on their part increases. There exists no mechanism for controlling their actions other than the potential threat to their next election, and the population at large has no other means of influencing the course of government. (By way of contrast, representatives in all other fields, such as law or commerce, cannot possess more rights than the people they represent, and they lose their mandate if they do not discharge their commission honestly.)

But the situation is paradoxical enough even without such comparisons. Thus, under the oft-encountered system whereby a government is formed by a parliamentary majority, members of this majority cease to function as independent spokesmen of the people vis-à-vis the government. Instead, they mobilize all their efforts to serve this government and to keep it in power at any cost. In other words, legislators become subordinate to the executive.

(It should also be said that the principle of total separation between executive, legislative, and judicial powers is not above criticism: does it not suggest fragmentation of a living state organism? The three separate powers need to operate within some unifying framework, perhaps an ethical rather than a structural one.)

There is the further point that the special demands of an election campaign require human qualities that have nothing in common with the qualities essential for leadership of a state. It would be rare for an individual to possess both sets of qualities, since the latter would be a handicap in the election contest.

Today, "representation" has become a kind of profession, virtually a lifelong career. There is a growing class of "professional politicians" for whom politics is an occupation and a means of livelihood. They are ever involved in intricate parliamentary maneuvers and there is little point in speaking about "the will of the people" in this context.

One is also struck by the preponderance of jurists and lawyers in most parliaments; one might designate it a "jurocracy." (Such a term is all the more appropriate since the plethora of laws and the complexity of legal procedures are such that an ordinary citizen is virtually incapable of defending himself before the law and needs the costly help of an attorney at every step of the way.)

HOW IT CAN TURN OUT

It is true that democratic systems allow for a close scrutiny of the actions of public officials, even though, surprisingly enough, contemporary democracies have amassed their own ponderous bureaucracies.

However, it is by no means always that a majority gives voice to its opinion even in a general election. In many cases, the vote is very light. In a number of Western countries, more than half, sometimes as many as two-thirds, of the voters do not show up at the polls, making the whole exercise rather meaningless. And the votes can fall in a way that a slim margin of victory can be attained by the addition of a tiny and insignificant party which will then in effect decide the fate of the country or its general course.

Semyon Frank foresaw this theoretical possibility long ago when he declared that democracies, too, are ruled by a minority. Vasili Rozanov expressed it as follows: "Democracy is a means whereby a well-organized minority holds sway over an unorganized majority."

Indeed, a flexible and smoothly working democracy is adept at deflecting popular protest and depriving it of any powerful outlet. Democracy, like other systems, is not immune to injustice, and dishonest individuals know how to evade responsibility. These kinds of machinations are dispersed among the agencies of the democratic bureaucracy to the point where they become impossible to track down. Anxious warnings have been sounded even in Switzerland, the world's oldest functioning democracy, concerning important decisions that are being made anonymously and without public scrutiny—somewhere behind the scenes, under the influence of lobbies and pressure groups (Hans Staub).

And even given equality of all persons before the law, there remains the actual inequality between the rich and the poor, which is to say the strong and the weak. (But it should be noted that the "poverty level" as it is understood in the contemporary West is much, much higher than what we imagine it to be.) As our political theorist Boris Chicherin pointed out in the nineteenth century, of all the varieties of aristocracy, one rises to the surface in a democratic system: the aristocracy of money. One cannot deny that money can bring real power in a democratic setting, and that an inevitable concentration of power occurs in the hands of those with large fortunes. In our country, too, the years of decaying socialism promoted an accumulation of such individuals in our "shadow economy," where they merged with the bureaucratic big shots; even in the years of "perestroika," they have managed to profit from the confusion of unclear laws and regulations. They are now at the starting lines and ready to begin public operations, so that it is all the more important that tight controls on any kind of monopoly be in place from the very beginning so as to prevent them from gaining power over us.

It is also depressing to note that the intellectual pseudo-elite engendered by the free-for-all of contemporary publicity ridicules the absolute nature of the concepts of good and evil, masking its indifference toward them by appeal to the "pluralism" of ideas and actions.

European democracy was originally imbued with a sense of Christian responsibility and self-discipline, but these spiritual principles have been gradually losing their force. Spiritual independence is being pressured on all sides by the dictatorship of self-satisfied vulgarity, of the latest fads, and of group interests.

We embark on democracy at a time when it is not at its healthiest.

POLITICAL PARTIES

We have today become incapable of imagining political life without parties, just as we cannot conceive of personal life without a family.

A month before the October coup, Trotsky offered the following pronouncement: "What is a party? It is a group of people attempting to gain power so as to implement its program. A party that does not wish to gain power does not deserve to be called a party."

Of course, the Bolshevik Party is a unique case. But the concept of party is very ancient, and its essence was understood early enough for the Roman historian Livy to write that "the struggle between parties is and will always remain a worse misfortune for the people than war, famine, plague, or any other manifestation of God's wrath."

The word "party" implies *part*. For us to be divided into parties thus means to be separated into parts. One might ask whom a party opposes in its role as a part of the people. This must evidently be all the rest of the people, those who did not choose to follow it. The efforts of every party are focused not on the welfare of the entire nation but on that of itself and its members. The national interest is eclipsed by party goals, above all on whatever the party needs to ensure its reelection. And should something useful to the state or the people have been proposed by a competing party, it is permissible to deny it support. The interests of parties, including their very existence, by no means coincide with the interests of the voters. Sergei Kryzhanovsky believed that the failings or even the collapse of parliamentary systems are directly brought on by parties that reject national unity and the very idea of patriotic feeling. The struggle between parties is not even remotely concerned with the search for truth: what is at stake is party prestige and wresting away some executive power. The top echelons of political parties are inevitably transformed into an oligarchy. And parties are responsible only to their own internal committees, since no outside controlling entity is stipulated under any constitution.

Party rivalry distorts the national will. The principle of party-mindedness necessarily involves the suppression of individuality, and every party reduces and coarsens the personal element. An individual will have views, while a party offers an ideology.

In this context, what kind of wish can be made for the future Russian Union?

No fundamental decisions affecting the state should be sought out along party paths, or handed over to the parties for resolution. An uncontrolled party fracas would spell disaster for our provinces and would deliver a final blow to our long-suffering rural areas. "Professional politicians" must not be allowed to substitute their voices for the voice of the nation. All professional expertise will be provided by a pool of public employees.

Parties of any kind, as well as any associations and unions, can exist freely, propounding any views and issuing publications at their own expense. But they must be open to public inspection and be registered, together with their programs. (Any secret organization, on the other hand, will be subject to criminal prosecution for conspiracy against society.) There will be no "party organizations" or other party interference in the workplace, in the service sector, or in the schools: all this must be beyond politics.

Parties, together with any other independent groups, have the right to nominate candidates for election to public office and to campaign on their behalf, but without drawing up party tickets: the vote must be for specific individuals, not parties. And an elected candidate must suspend any party membership for the duration of his term in office, assuming personal responsibility for his acts before his constituents. Power is a call to service, and it cannot be the subject of interparty competition.

Consequently, the formation of party groups is prohibited at all levels of government. And it goes without saying that the concept of a "ruling party" then ceases to exist.

THE DEMOCRACY OF SMALL AREAS

The critical comments about contemporary democracy expressed above are not meant to suggest that the future Russian Union will have no need for democracy. *It will need it very much.* But given our people's total lack of preparation for the intricacies of democratic life, democracy must be built from the bottom up, gradually, patiently, and in a way designed to last rather than being proclaimed thunderously from above in its full-fledged form.

All the failings noted earlier would rarely apply to democracies of small areas—mid-sized towns, small settlements [*poselki*], groups of villages [*volosti, stanitsy*], or areas up to the size of a county [*uyezd, rayon*]. Only in areas of this size can voters have confidence in their choice of candidates, since they will be familiar with them both in terms of their effectiveness in practical matters and in terms of their moral qualities. At this level, phony reputations do not hold up, nor would a candidate be helped by empty rhetoric or party sponsorship.

These are precisely the dimensions within which the new Russian democracy can begin to grow, gain strength, and acquire self-awareness. It also represents a level that is most certain to take root because it will involve the vital concerns of each locality: ensuring unpolluted water and air, overseeing housing, hospitals, nurseries, schools, shops, and the local distribution of goods, while also giving vigorous support to the growth of untrammeled local economic initiatives.

Without properly constituted local self-government, there can be no stable or prosperous life, and the very concept of civic freedom loses all meaning.

The democracy of small areas acquires its strength by being *unmeditated*. Democracy becomes genuinely effective in cases where citizens' assemblies can appropriately take the place of assemblies of representatives. The idea goes back to Athens and earlier, and such assemblies continue to function steadily in the United States, where they guide local affairs. I was fortunate to observe one such assembly in action in the Swiss canton of Appenzell. Although I have already described this episode elsewhere, I cannot resist giving a brief recapitulation here. Closely packed on the town square stood all those with a right to vote ("those capable of bearing arms," in Aristotle's formulation). Voting was conducted by an open show of hands. The head of the canton government, the Landammann, was reelected easily and with an obvious show of affection. But, of the bills he then introduced, three were immediately voted down. We trust you, the voters seemed to be saying, to govern us, but without those proposals.

In his policy speech, Landammann Broger spoke as follows: For more than five centuries our community has made no fundamental changes in the manner in which it governs itself. We are guided by the conviction that freedom is linked to our various responsibilities and to our self-restraint. There can be no freedom for the individual or the state without discipline and honesty. The people weigh and decide all important issues, but they cannot be present daily to run the state. For this reason, the process of governing will inevitably entail an admixture of the aristocratic and even monarchical modes. (Aristotle said the same thing.) The government, Broger went on, must not rush to keep up with fluctuating and ever-changeable popular opinion in order to get reelected, and it must not cajole voters with tempting rhetoric; it must, instead, move against the current. The goal of government should be to act in the way in which a rational majority of the people would act if they had all the facts before them—but the task is ever more difficult as the state becomes more and more overburdened. A democratic system, like no other, needs a strong hand to keep the ship of state on a steady and well-defined course.

Democracy of small areas had been practiced in Russia for centuries, with the peasant council [*mir*] existing throughout Russian history, while particular periods saw the *veche* assemblies and Cossack self-government.[35] Another example of this type of democracy was the *zemstvo*, an institution that had undergone substantial evolutionary development since its introduction in the nineteenth century.[36] Unfortunately, it existed only on the level of the district [*uyezd*] and province [*gubernia*], without being rooted in the villages [*volosti*] or rising to the all-Russian level. The October coup forcibly destroyed all *zemstvo* structures, replacing them with *soviets*,[37] which from the very beginning were subservient to the Communist Party. All our historical experience since 1918 discredits these *soviets*, which have never functioned as independent governing bodies at any level. Nor will the timid reforms of the electoral system now being undertaken be able to redeem the *soviets* as an institution: they do not ensure that local interests are communicated to the top. I hold that the "soviets of deputies" should be replaced slowly—step by step and from the bottom up—by a *zemstvo* system.

After many years of studying the history of the pre-revolutionary Russian state, I draw here on the legacy of our best statesmen and theoreticians, combining it with my own attempt at elaboration. It goes without saying that the experience of the past cannot simply be transplanted to the mutilated land of today, but it is also true that without reference to this background our recovery is unlikely to proceed in a healthy manner.

In this section of my essay I make use of a number of pre-revolutionary terms and concepts in order to avoid inventing new ones. Some of these terms will no doubt be replaced in common usage, others may survive.

THE ZEMSTVO

We shall distinguish four levels of the *zemstvo:*

· A *local zemstvo* (for a mid-sized town, a district in a large city, a settlement, or a group of villages)

· An *uyezd zemstvo* (for a large city, or for what is today called a *rayon*)

• An *oblast zemstvo* (for an *oblast* [region] or an Autonomous Republic)

• An *all-Russian* (or *all-Union*) *zemstvo*

For us who have completely lost touch with genuine self-government, the task will be to assimilate this sequence step by step, starting from the bottom. God preserve us from political wheelers and dealers, but it will be useful for many in the population to acquire political skills.

Voting will be for specific individuals only. In the context of a local *zemstvo,* the candidate will normally be well known to the voters. Election campaigns will preferably be short and modest affairs, involving nothing beyond a factual statement on each candidate's program, biography, and views. This procedure should not be funded by the state; local funding would be possible at the discretion of local authorities. Many other procedural details should likewise be decided locally, and they could differ substantially from region to region.

However, the following requirements would be mandatory everywhere.

1. An age requirement. What age must a voter attain to be allowed to participate in deciding the fate of the nation? In our time, adolescents do not have a stable upbringing, either in the family or in school, their education is superficial and haphazard, and some may demonstrate poor resistance to the most irresponsible of influences. Might it be a good idea therefore to raise the minimum age to twenty? (Localities or national districts may wish to set a still higher requirement.) Candidates for office would also have to meet an age requirement of perhaps thirty, or twenty-eight.

2. A residency requirement. Voters and especially elected officials must have roots in a given locality, they must understand its concerns and share its interests; recent arrivals or total strangers could not exercise responsible judgment here. Voters should be required to have resided locally for the preceding three years, without significant interruptions. (Localities may wish to increase this requirement.) For candidates, the minimum period of local residency should be the preceding five years (or, perhaps, the three preceding years plus five years at an earlier time).

An agreed-upon number of legislators will be elected to the local *zemstvo*. They will ratify administrative officials, who will be responsible to them on a continuing basis. In a rural district [*volost*] or a small settlement, this could be a single individual. At the next higher level, the *uyezd*, there would be the *uyezd* executive board [*uyezdnaya zemskaya uprava*], which would consist of individuals selected from the *uyezd* assembly [*uyezdnoe zemskoe sobranie*] or of specialists appointed by that body.

The newly elected *zemstvo* officials will take over the functions of the present local and district *soviets,* which will be abolished.

The local *zemstvo* will be elected by direct vote only, while in the case of the *uyezd* the voting procedure will depend on the size of the territory and the voters' familiarity with the candidates. If the area and the population density are both considerable, the more reliable method would be to proceed with two-stage elections: the local *zemstvos* would immediately replace the local *soviets* and would carry out their duties for half the regular term. Having reached that point, and with members now familiar with one another, they would elect an appropriate number from among themselves to the *uyezd zemstvo* to hold office until the next election. (During the first half of the term, the regional *soviets* [*raisovety*] and executive committees [*raiispolkomy*] would continue to function.)

Elections for the first (two-year?) term of office will be conducted at the local and *uyezd* levels only. Given our lack of political skills, the local and *uyezd zemstvo* organizations will serve as training ground as they perform the day-to-day tasks of governing our localities.

The process will begin shaping and bringing to the fore individuals with the potential for more challenging levels of service. One is impressed in this context by the example of the recently formed miners' strike committees as well as by the "unions of workers" which have displayed exceptional levels of awareness and organization.

STAGES IN THE TRANSFER OF POWER

Given the geographical immensity and the physical conditions of our country, direct elections of representatives to a central legislature could not be a productive exercise. Only three- or four-tier elections can ensure the seating of candidates with proven records and roots in their localities. Such elections would be based on long years of knowledge and trust rather than involving far-off and poorly known individuals with a recognition factor founded solely on the election campaign.

At the end of the first (or even second) term, elections will be held for the third (i.e., *oblast*) level of the *zemstvo* assembly. They will be carried out by the regional *uyezd* assemblies, together with the assembly of the main city in the region. A set number of representatives will be selected by these bodies from their own, now thoroughly familiar, ranks for service at the *oblast* level during the next term, whereupon the remaining *uyezd* assemblymen will stand for reelection.

An *oblast zemstvo* thus constituted will immediately replace the *oblast soviet* and will appoint an *oblast* executive board [*oblastnaya zemskaya uprava*] in lieu of the present *oblispolkom.* The *oblast* assembly will convene at set intervals, between which members will reside in their home districts. (After the system has begun to function reliably, the terms of office could be extended across the board.)

One should take into account here the advice of Dmitri Shipov, an outstanding figure in the pre-revolutionary *zemstvo* movement. To offset the possibility of erratic election results, Shipov suggested, an assembly should have the right to co-opt into its ranks (by full consensus, rather than a vote) prominent and urgently needed local figures, not exceeding one-fifth of its membership. In the conditions that will prevail in our country, such a procedure would provide the opportunity for successful members of the present-day *soviets* (including the Supreme Soviet) to be smoothly integrated into the new power structure.

The trust and respect earned by the *oblast zemstvo* will be directly proportional to the independence and self-reliance of Autonomous Republics and Autonomous Oblasts.

Without venturing to anticipate the future role of to-day's Supreme Soviets—those of the Russian Federation, the Ukraine, and Belorussia—it is natural to suggest that at the end of the following electoral term the assemblymen at the *oblast* level should select delegates from among their own number to the Union Chamber (replacing the Soviet of the Union) of the All-Zemstvo Assembly, which would replace the Supreme Soviet; the remaining *oblast*-level assemblymen would then stand for reelection by the *uyezd* assemblies according to the same principle.

The present system of two chambers, with equal power accorded to the Soviet of the Union [*Sovet Soyuza*] and the Soviet of Nationalities [*Sovet Natsionalnostei*],[38] would be quite satisfactory if it could be followed honestly and without pretense. The Chamber of Nationalities could be incorporated into an All-Zemstvo Assembly without any changes at all, except for the provision that each nationality would decide for itself the manner of filling the seats allocated to it, whether by general election or by appointment based on merit, as well as the length of the term involved.

The current Soviet of the Union is constituted according to an ill-defined and hybrid principle: some of the delegates are elected by means of territorial voting, others are appointed by the Communist Party and its various organizations. This is unacceptable even for the six- or four-year period of transition, and ways must be found to correct it. Moreover, it is a cumbersome structure further weighed down by the Congress of People's Deputies,[39] which results in needless complexity and duplication in legislative work.

Building a successful *zemstvo* system culminating in an All-Zemstvo Assembly requires the *zemstvo* assemblies at the *uyezd* and *oblast* levels to have gained considerable know-how in the course of their work, and for the *oblast* assemblymen to be able to select well-tested delegations from their ranks to the All-Zemstvo Assembly, delegations in which *oblast*-level experience would combine with a national perspective and would always be represented in it. A parliament must not be an abstract "central" entity; it should always consist of authoritative regional representatives who would in addition be required to reside a certain part of the year in their home district so as not to lose their right to represent it. (Such a rule also exists in the United States.)

A COMBINED SYSTEM OF GOVERNMENT

What is meant here is a rational way for the centralized bureaucracy to collaborate with grass-roots public activity.

This kind of partnership existed during certain periods in Muscovite Russia, with local self-government involving itself with local affairs and also partially with national ones, albeit under the supervision of the central authorities.

In 1899 Sergei Witte[40] restrained Nicholas II from granting increased rights to the *zemstvo* organizations by presenting the fallacious argument that autocracy was incompatible with broad local self-rule. (Soon thereafter, Lev Tikhomirov, a former member of the "People's Will" group turned monarchist, refuted this argument, but was not heard.)

A centralized bureaucracy by its very nature tries to restrict the sphere of society's self-management. This, however, is necessary only for the bureaucracy; it is certainly not needed by the people, nor is it necessary for the government. In healthy times, the public hungers for activity, and the broadest possible opportunities should be made available for this urge. As Tikhomirov phrased it, wherever the public is capable of maintaining necessary standards by itself, any action by state agencies is superfluous and even harmful, to the extent that it needlessly weakens the people's habit of self-reliance. Access to direct public activity should be open wherever such activity is appropriate, whether it is manifested in local self-government or in associations and unions.

Furthermore, the cooperation of the public is an indispensable help in controlling the central bureaucracy and ensuring that its officials will perform honest and efficient service.

This type of combined system, a kind of working partnership between the state bureaucracy and the administration of local self-governing units, was termed by Shipov the *state-zemstvo system.*

However, in the current period of transition (which may not be short) we can expect a different relationship between these two centers of power. While the grassroots social forces are slowly gathering strength, acquiring experience, and shaping the leaders of tomorrow, the present-day bureaucracy, with its habit of unchecked power, will do all it can to cling to its rights. Nevertheless, a sharp reduction of these rights is imminent with the arrival of economic independence in the country. And the constructive forces that are already coming to light in today's freshly elected, transitional *soviets* will help the movement toward an ever-broader social independence.

CONCERNING THE CENTRAL AUTHORITIES

Given the vastness of our country and the multitude of its problems, it is today by no means inappropriate to have a strong presidency. However, all the prerogatives of the head of state together with the manner of dealing with potential conflicts must be rigorously stipulated by law; this is all the more applicable to the procedure of electing the President. He will acquire genuine legitimacy only after being elected by national vote to a term of five or perhaps seven years. This election, however, should not become an occasion for wasting the energies of the nation on a vehement and slanted campaign lasting weeks or months where the paramount goal is smearing one's opponent. It would suffice for the All-Zemstvo Assembly to nominate several native-born candidates, resident in the country during the preceding seven or ten years. The Assembly would subject these candidates to a thorough review and would then issue public statements of equal length on each, stating the basis for its findings, together with a summary of any dissenting views. The subsequent popular vote (conducted in one or two rounds, to ensure an absolute majority) could then avoid an intense and exhausting election campaign. (It would probably be wise to follow the American model in establishing the office of Vice-President as well, with the candidate for this post being chosen by the presidential aspirant, and the two running as a team.)

If during the President's term in office three-quarters of both chambers of the All-Zemstvo Assembly determine that the President is discharging his duties unsatisfactorily, the Assembly will publish a documented statement to this effect, submitting it to a popular vote, together with possible new candidacies. If, on the contrary, the Assembly votes its continuing support for a president at the expiration of his term, by a two-thirds majority in each chamber, there would seem to be no reason not to extend his tenure for another term without a new national election. If the President should die in office during the second half of his term, the Vice President will assume his post until the end of the term; if he dies during the first half, a new national election will be held.

The President will appoint a Council of Ministers at his discretion. They will preferably be specialists inducted into government service on a competitive basis; it would not be desirable to draw on members of the legislative assemblies. The ministers will report to the President as well as to both chambers of the Assembly, but they will not be removable by the legislature. (One might consider here the suggestion made by Pyotr Stolypin in a memorandum prepared shortly before his death: instituting a two- or three-year academy for those aspiring to top government posts. Such an academy would admit individuals of outstanding promise who had graduated with distinction from institutions of higher

learning and could present strong personal or institu-
tional recommendations. Courses of study would reflect
the concerns of the ministries, and Stolypin laid particular emphasis on one designed to help local self-rule.)

As the legal scholar Viktor Leontovich defined it, a
government differs from an administration (in the sense
of a bureaucracy) by having to solve *new* problems,
while an administration deals only with familiar and con-
ventional ones. This is the reason ministers must be so
highly qualified, and if a government slips into a bureaucratic mode of thinking, it will lose its ability to lead the
nation.

At the same time, work within the administration system must not be viewed as a reward or special privilege,
and it must not be tied to any personal advantage. "The
only productive government is one that regards itself
solely in terms of its responsibilities," noted Mikhail
Katkov. After all the things we have had to experience,
every kind of authority is by definition indebted to the
people. To the present task of rebuilding and making up
for all that has been destroyed, government agencies
must dedicate all their efforts, perhaps instituting a
longer workday.

There are not many ways in which we can emulate
Switzerland, given that country's size and the history of
its formation as a union of independent cantons. But we

can certainly borrow one idea: a petition that collects a certain number of signatures is introduced into the legislature, where it must be reviewed; if the number of signatures is considerably greater (in our case this would be in the millions), a plebiscite on the question becomes mandatory. Such legislative initiatives from the grass-roots level inject flexibility into the conduct of state affairs.

Apart from such plebiscites and the infrequent presidential elections, no other national elections would be necessary.

A CONSULTATIVE BODY

This chapter is not meant to be applicable to the present moment; I append it here because I think it may have great importance for the distant future of our state.

Reflecting on his rich experience in the Duma, Vasili Maklakov stressed that the most durable achievements of a democratic system derive from agreements between the majority and the minority, rather than from a preponderance of the former over the latter. For countries lacking in political experience, he even suggested a *third* parliamentary chamber, consisting of "an experienced and highly educated minority"; although this would create an impediment to the unchecked spread of democracy, he thought it would ultimately be less of a danger to democracy than the uncontrolled power of the majority.

To carry Maklakov's idea a step further, it would seem that we must seek a loftier form for decisions of state than what is provided by the simple mechanisms of a vote. To decide everything by majority vote means to establish a dictatorship of the majority over the minority and over those *dissenting opinions* which are particularly valuable in the search for new paths of development.

High standards in all the undertakings of governing authorities cannot be attained without establishing ethical controls over them. This could be accomplished by a supreme moral entity endowed with an advisory role—a kind of institution that would not typically resort to voting but would instead present in-depth arguments and counterarguments offered by the most respected authorities upon whom the state could draw.

Our history offers a reliable model in the Assembly of the Land [*Zemskii Sobor*] of Muscovite Russia.[41] Dmitri Shipov has written that these assemblies did not occasion struggles between the Tsar and the Assembly. There is no recorded instance of the Tsar acting contrary to the Assembly's judgment, because differing with the Assembly would only undermine the Tsar's authority. *Sobornost*[42] is a system of trust which is based on the assumption that moral unity is both possible and achievable.

The idea might be possible to realize in a Duma (perhaps "State Duma" or "Sobor Duma") constituted in a way that could be said to reflect the national conscience: an assembly of highly respected individuals of lofty moral character, wisdom, and rich experience. But the trouble with this idea is that there seems to be no clear method of choosing such individuals.

To a certain extent, this goal could be realized by substituting a Duma consisting of representatives of social strata and various professions, or, one might say, "estates" [*soslovia*]. (Vladimir Dal's primary definition of the word *soslovie* is: a group of people with a common occupation having the same legal rights; the second definition adds: category, class, and caste.)

The two most natural conditions promoting interaction and cooperation among people are a shared territory and a common occupation or type of activity. Each of us has his work and his specialty which allows us to be useful members of society. Complete and faceless equality in this context would amount to entropy and a step toward death. A society lives precisely by virtue of its differentiation. The burden of the state is borne by those who think, work, and create everything the nation lives by. The better organized society is within its social groupings, the greater will be its output of creative energy (Lev Tikhomirov).

With time, our newly unshackled society will undoubtedly see the emergence of creative "estates" in this sense of groupings by profession and specialty. For much too long, everything in our country has been under the control of people who had not the slightest understanding of the enterprises they were managing. Control will finally be turned over to individuals with real knowledge. And no one is better equipped to offer advice about a specific project than a representative of the specialty in question. (Estates based on the common creative impulse that gives unity to the spiritual and professional lives of people in the same specialty must not be confused with trade unions. In the case of estates as defined above, one automatically becomes a member simply by virtue of one's profession, while a trade union is an organization designed to fight for higher wages and other benefits; membership is optional and controlled by the union.)

Beyond the *zemstvo* representation based on the territorial principle, then, we could see the emergence of representation by estate. (And part of the energy that is now fruitlessly expended on political parties would be turned toward the constructive end of developing the estates.)

Every estate would determine the procedure whereby its delegates would be elected or appointed to the Duma. This would not be a matter of choosing political deputies or of charging them with the task of defending the estate's political interests; rather, the estates would select experienced and respected individuals who could be trusted to express the general views of the group.

To keep the work focused, the size of this Duma should not exceed 200 or 250 delegates. (If the number of estates turns out to be greater than that, one delegate could represent a group of related small estates.)

An opinion rendered without a vote is by no means a new idea. Thus, the mountain people of the Caucasus have long followed the procedure of "polling the wise men," in lieu of a general vote.

Any opinion, judgment, or request for information, fully substantiated and addressed to the President, to the Council of Ministers, to either chamber of the Assembly, or to the Supreme Court by more than half of the Duma will be published. And the person or body so addressed will be obligated to respond positively or to publish the reasons for non-compliance within a two-week period. (In exceptional cases involving military secrets, the exchange will be carried out behind closed doors, but members of the Duma will continue to have full access to any necessary information bearing on the activity of the President, the government, the legislature, or the courts.)

A candidate for the presidency can likewise be nominated by a similar majority of the Duma.

And whenever the Duma's judgment is expressed *unanimously*, it will have the power to interdict any law or any action by a government institution or agency, and to mandate changes or corrections. In the same manner, the Duma will have the power to veto any candidacy for the office of President.

The addition of a consultative and highly knowledgeable Duma will have a direct moral and intellectual impact on all facets of government, whereas the potential for improving society by exclusively political means is not very great.

"The purpose of life in society is to establish a moral order among people" (Mikhail Speransky). "For freedom and the rule of law to endure, they must be rooted in the consciousness of the people" (Aleksei K. Tolstoy). "Political stability endures only when it is founded on moral strength" (Vasili Klyuchevsky).

Laws designate the minimum moral standards below which an individual represents a danger to society.

"There are many instances when what is right under the law is prohibited by morality, which imposes higher and stricter demands upon man" (Pavel Novgorodtsev).

Moral principles must take priority over legal ones. And justice means conformity to moral law beyond any purely legal compliance.

LET US SEARCH

In this brief essay I was unable to touch upon the army, the militia, the courts, the trade unions, or most legislative and economic issues. My purpose was simply to offer a number of proposals, none of which lay claim to finality, so as to prepare the ground for discussion.

Building a rational and just state order is a task of surpassing difficulty, and the goal can only be approached slowly by means of successive approximations and small, cautious steps. This task has not been achieved even in the thriving lands of the West (which we must regard with eyes clear of rapture), but it will be infinitely more difficult and painful for us, starting as we do with a country in catastrophic ruin and a population deprived of the habits and skills of a viable society.

It is impossibly difficult to design a balanced plan for future action; there is every likelihood that it will contain more errors than virtues and that it will be unable to keep pace with the actual unfolding of events. But it would also be wrong not to make the effort.

The present essay is based on the reflections of numerous Russian thinkers of the past, and my hope is that bringing their thoughts together here will contribute to a vigorous new growth.

July 1990[43]

NOTES

[ANNOTATIONS HAVE BEEN PREPARED BY THE TRANSLATOR]

1. "Patriotic War" is the Soviet term for the conflict with Nazi Germany in 1941–45.

2. In the order referred to, the eleven are: Estonia, Latvia, Lithuania; Georgia, Armenia, Azerbaijan; Uzbekistan, Tadjikistan, Kirghizia, Turkmenia; and Moldavia (Moldova). That leaves four Union Republics of the fifteen that make up the U.S.S.R.: the Russian Federated Republic [R.S.F.S.R.], Ukraine, Belorussia, and Kazakhstan.

3. Nagorno-Karabakh, formally an Autonomous Oblast within Azerbaijan, is populated primarily by Armenians, and has been the scene of violent ethnic conflict between Armenians and Azerbaijanis. The borders were drawn in 1923, a time when Lenin's government was giving substantial support to the Atatürk regime in Turkey. Turks and Azerbaijanis are culturally and linguistically related.

4. Autonomous Republics are Soviet territorial units based loosely on the national identity of the indigenous population but deemed not large or important enough to acquire Union Republic status.

5. Exiled peoples included the Volga Germans, deported *en masse* to Central Asia in 1941 as alleged security risks, and several nationalities banished from their home territories for purported collaboration with, or sympathy for, the wartime enemy. Kazakhstan was also the site of an immense complex of forced-labor camps.

6. Whereas the adjective *russkii* is applied only to Great Russians, the term *rossiiskii* used here suggests a broader definition that permits the inclusion of other ethnic groups. (The distinction is similar to that between "English" and "British.")

7. The overwhelming majority of these national groups reside within the boundaries of the present R.S.F.S.R.

8. Poland and Finland were part of the Russian Empire until 1917.

9. The Mongols overran most of the principalities of Kievan Rus in the mid-thirteenth century. As Mongol control disintegrated in the westernmost of these areas, the lands now known as Ukraine and Belorussia fell under Lithuanian and then Polish control for three, and in some cases four, centuries.

10. The earliest historical account of Kievan Rus is contained in the *Primary Chronicle,* compiled by the monk Nestor at the beginning of the twelfth century.

11. Yaroslav the Wise and Vladimir Monomakh were outstanding rulers of Kievan Rus in the eleventh and twelfth centuries, respectively.

12. The Ukrainian Central Rada [i.e., Council], formed in Kiev soon after the collapse of tsarist authority, was a coalition of groups seeking Ukrainian territorial autonomy.

13. The reference is to Public Law 86–90, passed in 1959, which requires the President to proclaim a yearly "Captive Nations Week." The preamble contains language equating communism with Russian imperialism.

14. Vladimir, Prince of Kiev (956–1015), was canonized for bringing Christianity to what was then called Rus. The term Ukraine began to be used in its present geographical meaning only several centuries later.

15. "New Russia" is the former name of the territories north of the Black Sea and the Sea of Azov which were acquired by Russia (mostly in the eighteenth century) in its wars with Turkey. The Crimean peninsula—historically part of "New Russia"—was transferred from the R.S.F.S.R to the Ukrainian Republic in 1954 at the whim of Nikita Khrushchev. The Donbas industrial area has a predominantly Russian-speaking population.

16. The Soviet of Nationalities is one of the two chambers making up the U.S.S.R. Supreme Soviet. Union Republics, Autonomous Republics, Autonomous Oblasts, and National Okrugs each send a specified number of delegates to this body (thirty-two, eleven, five, and one, respectively).

17. In 1944 the Crimean Tatars were deported to Central Asia for their alleged collaboration with the Germans. Their persistent attempts to return to the Crimea became a noticeable factor in the dissident movement of the 1960s and 1970s.

18. The Abkhazian Autonomous Republic and the Southern Ossetian Autonomous Oblast are both within the Georgian Republic. Meskhetian Turks, a largely Moslem and linguistically Turkicized group within Georgia, were exiled to Central Asia after World War II.

19. Article Six of the Soviet Constitution had guaranteed a monopoly of power to the Communist Party of the Soviet Union. The article was repealed in 1990.

20. The Russian Communist Party was established in 1990. There had previously been no Communist Party organization specific to the R.S.F.S.R.

21. Pyotr Stolypin (1862–1911), Russian Prime Minister between 1906 and 1911, had instituted agrarian reforms designed to break up the peasant communes by encouraging the private ownership of land.

22. The first of several Five-Year Plans covered the years 1928–33 and entailed the forced collectivization of agriculture.

23. Mikhail Lomonosov (1711–65), a brilliantly gifted boy from a northern village, made his way to Moscow and in time became a leading scientist and the founder of Moscow University.

24. The 1917 February Revolution brought about the abdication of Tsar Nicholas II and the establishment of a so-called Provisional Government which shared power with the socialist-controlled Soviets of Workers' and Soldiers' Deputies. In the eight chaotic months between February and the Bolshevik coup of October, the Provisional Government demonstrated a distressing lack of political realism.

25. The criticism of the tsarist government's war policies and of the royal family's public image reached a crescendo in late 1916.

26. Vyacheslav Molotov (1890–1986), a long-time member of the Politburo, was for many years the head of Stalin's foreign-affairs establishment. The many services to Stalin's regime of Lazar Kaganovich (1893–1991) included the suppression of nationalist uprisings; he also played a major role in the forced collectivization campaign of the 1930s. (Kaganovich was still alive at the time Solzhenitsyn's essay appeared in Russian.)

27. Jan Berzin (1881–1938), a Latvian Communist, became one of the principal organizers of, and administrators in, the Soviet forced-labor-camp system. There has been talk of erecting a monument to him in Magadan, in northeastern Siberia, where some of the most notorious camps were located.

28. This is the official Soviet cliché launched in the Gorbachev era to characterize the period under Brezhnev.

29. Solzhenitsyn's term for educated persons lacking moral perspective and broad intellectual vision. See his essay with this title in the collection *From Under the Rubble*.

30. This practice involves the physical abuse and systematic humiliation of new army recruits by soldiers in their last year of duty. Severe beatings and frequent suicides have been reported.

31. In the period immediately after the fall of the monarchy, the Russian Orthodox Church briefly adopted the practice (followed in the Early Church) of selecting its hierarchs

by means of a vote involving both clergy and laity. Bishop Veniamin and Archbishop Tikhon were elected Metropolitans of Petrograd and Moscow, respectively. A few months later the Church Council elected Tikhon to the post of Patriarch.

32. Elected by democratic vote in November of 1917, the Constituent Assembly met in Petrograd on January 18, 1918, but was dispersed the next day by armed Bolshevik sailors when it refused to cede power to the Bolshevik regime. (The Bolsheviks had managed to win only a quarter of the seats in the Assembly.)

33. If the Constituent Assembly could have been convened before the Bolsheviks had consolidated their power, the moderate parties that represented the majority would have been in a position to assert control.

34. The State Duma was a representative assembly established by statute in 1905. There were four Dumas before 1917: the first two were dissolved in 1906 and 1907; the third and fourth were in session in 1907–12 and 1912–17, respectively.

35. The *veche,* a town assembly in medieval Russia, was an example of direct democracy. Developed most fully in Novgorod and Pskov, the *veche* functioned as a continuing institution for almost four hundred years. The internal organization of Cossack groups was also based on direct elections. Cossack communities were at the height of their power in the sixteenth and seventeenth centuries.

36. The *zemstvo* as an institution of local self-rule was established in 1864. It dealt with matters like roads, irrigation,

public education, and medical services, but with time its leaders became progressively more involved in broad policy issues.

37. *Soviets* first emerged during the 1905 Revolution as committees to coordinate strike activity and armed insurrection. They resurfaced in 1917 and were at first dominated by socialists. Lenin wrested control of the Petrograd Soviet in late 1917 and since then *soviets* have been institutionalized at all levels of government. While they are meant to demonstrate popular control of the system, they are in reality entirely ineffective in representing local interests.

38. The Soviet of the Union consists mostly of delegates elected in proportion to the population (one deputy for 300,000 voters). Other delegates are appointed. On the Soviet of Nationalities, see Note 16 above.

39. The Congress of People's Deputies is a kind of "super-parliament" established in the Gorbachev era. Its most significant accomplishment has been the in-house election of Gorbachev as President in 1990.

40. Count Sergei Witte (1849–1915), Russian Minister of Finance, 1892–1903; Prime Minister, 1903–6.

41. *Sobors* of this kind date from the sixteenth century, with the most notable being the one that installed the Romanov dynasty on the Russian throne in 1613.

42. The concept of *sobornost* refers to the kind of spirit that prompts freely offered agreement. It has been defined as expressing "unity in multiplicity."

43. This essay was published in two Soviet newspapers, *Komsomolskaya pravda* and *Literaturnaya gazeta* (both on September 18, 1990), with a note specifying that the fee due the author had at his request been turned over to a fund for the victims of Chernobyl.

APPENDIX

This alphabetical appendix, compiled by the translator, provides brief information on non-Western thinkers, writers, and political figures whose views have been referred to in the text.

Chicherin, Boris Nikolaevich (1828–1904)
Historian, philosopher, and major figure in the history of Russian liberalism. Chicherin considered constitutional monarchy the system of choice for Russia, rejecting the two central tenets of the Russian politicized opposition: the idealization of the peasant commune typical of the populists, and the blind faith in the violent transformations envisioned by revolutionaries.

Dal, Vladimir Ivanovich (1801–72)
Writer and lexicographer. His four-volume *Dictionary* (1863–66) is an unsurpassed source of the popular idiom, proverbial expressions, and dialectical usage; it is much admired by Solzhenitsyn.

Dragomanov (Drahomanov), Mikhail Petrovich
(1841–95)
Ukrainian historian and political theorist who championed autonomy for the Ukraine but believed this would be best achieved within the framework of a federative union with

Russia. Dragomanov firmly opposed political extremism of any kind, including national chauvinism. Lived abroad after 1876.

Fedotov, Georgi (George) Petrovich (1886–1951)
Historian, essayist, and religious thinker with leftist, but firmly anti-communist, political views. After emigrating in 1925, held academic posts in France and the U.S.

Frank, Semyon Lyudvigovich (1877–1950)
Prominent philosopher, one of the contributors to a famous 1909 collection of essays (*Vekhi*) criticizing the doctrinaire mind-set of the Russian radical intelligentsia. After expulsion from Russia in 1922, Frank lived in Germany, France, and England.

Gessen, Iosif Vladimirovich (1866–1943)
Essayist and liberal politician. One of the founders of the Constitutional Democratic Party (1905), Gessen was closely aligned with Pavel Milyukov. Editor of influential St. Petersburg daily *Rech,* and later of a twenty-two-volume set of primary materials bearing on the Russian Revolution.

Ilyin, Ivan Aleksandrovich (1883–1954)
Philosopher and essayist. After his expulsion from Russia in 1922, Ilyin devoted much of his effort to an active struggle against Bolshevism, all the while remaining highly critical of the failings of the old regime. In 1925 he published a widely noted philosophical justification of physical resistance to evil.

Katkov, Mikhail Nikiforovich (1818–87)
Journalist and acerbic conservative essayist. A highly successful editor of the monthly *Russkii vestnik,* Katkov pub-

lished many of the celebrated novels of Tolstoy, Dostoevsky, and Turgenev. Katkov's political views have many points in common with those of nineteenth-century British Tories.

Klyuchevsky, Vasili Osipovich (1841–1911)

Long-time professor at Moscow University and the most renowned historian of Russia. Klyuchevsky's historical analyses are notable for their careful attention to social, economic, and cultural factors.

Kryzhanovsky, Sergei Efimovich (1862–1934)

High official in the Ministry of Interior, specializing in local economic development. Later, assistant to Stolypin and author of electoral law for Duma elections. Between 1911 and 1917, head of the chancellery of the State Council. Left Russia in 1920.

Leontovich (Leontovitsch), Viktor Vladimirovich (1902–59)

Historian, author of a ground-breaking study on the history of Russian liberalism. Held academic posts in Germany.

Levitsky, Sergei Aleksandrovich (1908–83)

Philosopher and essayist, author of an important treatise on the philosophical meaning of freedom. Held academic posts in the U.S.

Maklakov, Vasili Alekseevich (1869–1957)

Jurist and member of the moderate wing of the Constitutional Democratic Party. In his legislative career as a member of the Duma, Maklakov eschewed the confrontational tactics favored by many other delegates, seeking ways of constructive compromise within a legal framework. Left Russia in 1917.

Milyukov, Pavel Nikolaevich (1859–1943)
Historian and head of the Constitutional Democratic Party. An uncompromising exponent of the liberal creed, Miliukov tended to use the Duma rostrum more for attacks on the government than for constructive legislative activity. Left Russia in 1920.

Novgorodtsev, Pavel Nikolaevich (1866–1924)
Liberal philosopher and legal scholar who attempted to formulate philosophical principles upon which a just social structure could be based, one that would take account of twentieth-century realities. Expelled from Russia in 1920.

Rozanov, Vasili Vasilyevich (1856–1919)
Writer of aphoristic prose, literary critic, philosopher, and master of paradox.

Shipov, Dmitri Nikolaevich (1851–1920)
Chairman of the prestigious Moscow *zemstvo* board and tireless promoter of the cause of local self-rule, Shipov at the same time tried to avoid conflict with the autocratic system. Influenced by the Slavophile notion of "unity in multiplicity," he believed that the task of politics was to reconcile the views of all major political forces.

Shuvalov, Count Pyotr Ivanovich (1711–62)
Influential counselor to Empress Elizabeth of Russia and high-ranking military officer.

Solovyov, Vladimir Sergeevich (1853–1900)
Poet, mystic, and preeminent Russian philosopher, Solovyov provided the major impetus for the religious and phil-

osophical renaissance that Russia experienced at the turn
of the century. Solovyov was a forceful critic of Russian
nationalist chauvinism.

Speransky, Count Mikhail Mikhailovich (1772–1839)
As a high official under Tsar Alexander I, Speransky
drafted an ambitious plan for reforming Russia's judicial and
administrative institutions; the scheme included a call for
the establishment of an elected legislature and of local self-
rule. But Speransky fell into disfavor and the plan was not
implemented. In later years he undertook the enormous
task of codifying the existing Russian laws.

Tikhomirov, Lev Aleksandrovich (1852–1923)
A radical populist and committed member of a terrorist organization, Tikhomirov underwent a conversion in 1888,
renouncing his revolutionary views and becoming a leading
right-wing journalist.

Tolstoy, Aleksei Konstantinovich (1817–75)
Poet, playwright, and novelist whose best-known works
are based on sixteenth- and seventeenth-century Russian
history.

Uspensky, Gleb Ivanovich (1843–1903)
Writer and journalist. A major figure in the history of Russian populism, Uspensky is noted mainly for his sketches
and stories of peasant life.